Columbia University

Contributions to Education

Teachers College Series

No. 15

AMS PRESS
NEW YORK

Public Education in Upper Canada

BY

Herbert Thomas John Coleman

PUBLISHED BY
TEACHERS COLLEGE
COLUMBIA UNIVERSITY
NEW YORK
1907

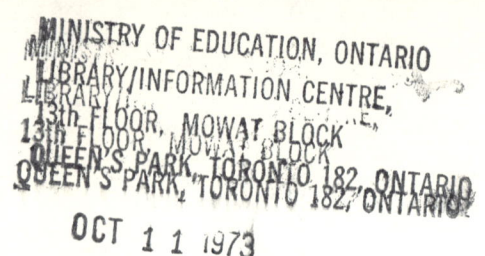

OCT 1 1 1973

Library of Congress Cataloging in Publication Data

Coleman, Herbert Thomas John, 1872— Jan 20, Jun 10, 1964
  Public education in upper Canada.

  Original ed. issued as no. 15 of Columbia University Contributions to education, Teachers College series.
  Originally presented as the author's thesis, Columbia.
  Bibliography: p.
  1. Education—Ontario. I. Title. II. Series: Columbia University. Teachers College. Contributions to education, no. 15.
  LA418.O6C58 1972   379.713   78-176661
  ISBN 0-404-55015-0
  ISBN 0-404-55000-2 (set)

Reprinted by Special Arrangement with Teachers College Press, Columbia University, New York

From the edition of 1907: New York
First AMS edition published in 1972
Manufactured in the United States

AMS PRESS, INC.
NEW YORK, N.Y. 10003

CONTENTS.

CHAPTER I..Page 9
THE POLITICAL AND SOCIAL BACKGROUND
Purpose of chapter.— Early conditions; French military posts; French settlers in Upper Canada prior to 1791.— The Loyalist emigration; nationalities represented; assistance furnished by British Government; the chief Loyalist settlements.— Later emigration from the United States.— Emigration from Europe; almost wholly from the British Isles; segregation of race elements; one notable exception; unfortunate result of the policy of segregation.—Abuses in the granting of land; Judge Thorpe's criticisms, 1807; Mr. Gourlay's investigations, 1817-18; cumulative effect of Government's policy.— The structure and character of the Provincial Government; large powers of Executive; slight powers possessed by House of Assembly; chief functions of the latter body.— Municipal organization of the Province; the District; the County; the Township; the School District.— Religious denominations; contemporary accounts of numerical standing and privileges enjoyed; the struggle for equal rights; the Clergy Reserves; the right to solemnize marriage.— General conditions of life; roads; traveling; communication with Great Britain; newspapers; post-offices.— Conclusion.

CHAPTER II..Page 21
THE LAND GRANTS FOR SCHOOLS
Educational policy of Lieutenant-Governor John Graves Simcoe, 1792-1796; his correspondence with the British Government; the defects of his policy.— The Royal Land Grant of 1797; its chief provisions.— University the earliest and chief beneficiary from Land Grant; reasons therefor; the Reverend John Strachan and his influence in Provincial politics.— Steps taken to dispose of School lands for University purposes; action of Executive Council, 1819; exchange of University lands for more valuable Crown Reserves, 1827; value of University Endowment, 1839-1842.— Endowment from University lands of "National" Schools and Upper Canada College.—Action of House of Assembly, 1831, looking to the realization of a fund for Grammar and Common Schools; failure of that body to appreciate difficulties of the situation; report of the Executive Council on School Lands, 1831; 250,000 acres granted to Grammar Schools, 1839.— Movement for a special endowment for Common Schools; legislative proceedings in this regard, 1816, 1831, 1832, 1833; recommendations of Lieutenant-Governor, 1835; failure of Common School Endowment Bill, 1839; eventual success of movement, 1849.— Effect on educational legislation of the political complications of the time.

Contents.

CHAPTER III..Page 33
THE DISTRICT GRAMMAR SCHOOL — LEGISLATIVE AND ADMINISTRATIVE ASPECTS

Legislative proceedings prior to 1807.— The District (Grammar) School Act of 1807; its chief provisions; Act made permanent in 1808; popular dissatisfaction with the Act as reflected in proceedings of the House of Assembly, 1808-1816; the Common School Act of 1816 a concession to this popular sentiment; continued agitation against the act, 1817-1819.— The District Grammar School Amendment Act, 1819; analysis of its contents.— Founding of new Grammar Schools, 1819-1839.— The General Board of Education (1823-1833) in its relations to the Grammar Schools. — Grammar Schools under the direction of the Council of King's College, 1833-1841.— Changes in administration of Grammar Schools introduced by Act of 1839.— The union of Upper and Lower Canada, 1841, and the Grammar School Act of that year.— General attitude of the Provincial Government towards Grammar Schools during the period under consideration.

CHAPTER IV..Page 44
THE DISTRICT GRAMMAR SCHOOL — ITS PECULIAR FEATURES

The Reverend John Strachan, the most famous of the Grammar School masters; his connection with the schools at Cornwall and York; his thoroughness; his fondness for scientific study; his advocacy of a liberal curriculum; his methods as a teacher.— Later masters of the Grammar School at York; Mr. Samuel Armour; the Reverend Thomas Phillips.— Conditions in other Grammar Schools of the Province; the Midland District Grammar School (at Kingston); the Eastern District Grammar School (at Cornwall); the Ottawa District Grammar School; the Western District Grammar School (at Sandwich); the Johnstown District Grammar School (at Brockville).— Characteristics of the Grammar School as an institution.— Upper Canada College, the "superior" Grammar School at York; its distinguishing features; its value as supplying, for the time being, the place of a University; its limitations; its history subsequent to 1841.

CHAPTER V...Page 55
THE COMMON SCHOOL — ITS EXTERNAL HISTORY

No provision for elementary schools in the Land Grant of 1797.— Beginnings of elementary education in the Province; Garrison Schools; other private schools, 1789-1810.— Early certification of teachers.— An early petition for Government aid of elementary schools.— The Common School Act of 1816; its chief provisions; defects of the Act.— The Common School Act of 1820.— The Common School Act of 1824; provision for Sunday Schools; recognition of a General Board of Education; facts concerning this body; chief cause of its discontinuance.— Increase of annual grant to Common Schools, 1835.— Unsuccessful Common School Bills introduced in House of Assembly, 1830-1840; Mr. William Buell, Jr.'s

Bill; Mr. Mahlon Burwell's Bill; visit of Dr. Charles Duncombe to the United States; his report and draft of a Common School Bill.— The Common School Act of 1841; its chief provisions.— Subsequent legislation.

CHAPTER VI ....Page 68

THE COMMON SCHOOL — ITS ESSENTIAL CHARACTERISTICS

Incompleteness of data at hand.— Schools in keeping with pioneer conditions.— Pioneer life, as a whole, unfavorable to formal education.— Some compensating features; Dr. Bourinot quoted.— Some early schoolhouses; description (1818) of the school buildings of the time.— Leading types of the early schoolmaster.— Prevalence of American teachers; attitude towards them by the authorities; characterization of them by writers of the time.— The Common School curriculum and text-books; scarcity of the latter; methods of instruction; daily program of the Common School at York, 1821.—American text-books in the schools; agitation against them; their eventual exclusion.— Efforts of the General Board of Education to meet the local need.— Chief cause of the low state of the Common Schools during this period.

CHAPTER VII ....Page 79

THE RELIGIOUS FACTOR IN PUBLIC EDUCATION — THE GRAMMAR AND THE COMMON SCHOOLS

General belief in Upper Canada in the necessity of religious instruction in the schools; difference of opinion as to the form it should take; "Separate Schools" the answer, so far as the Roman Catholics are concerned; gradual relaxing of religious requirement in Common Schools attended by Protestants.

The Church of England and the Grammar Schools; charge of Anglican domination made by the United Presbytery of Upper Canada in 1830; reply of a Committee of the Legislative Council; the Presbytery reiterates its charges; confessedly Anglican character of Upper Canada College.

The Church of England and the Common Schools; a Provincial system of Church of England National Schools projected, 1820; Royal approval of the plan, 1823; introduction of the systems of both Bell and Lancaster in Upper Canada; details of the establishment of the Central National School at York; the Appleton Case; Parliamentary investigation and report; continuation of the Central National School till 1844.

Conclusion; the Appleton Case illustrates but one phase of the struggle going on in the Province at the time.

CHAPTER VIII ....Page 91

THE RELIGIOUS FACTOR IN PUBLIC EDUCATION — THE PROVISIONAL UNIVERSITY

The two chief parties in the University controversy.— The University Charter of 1827; Dr. Strachan's visit to England; his "Appeal" on behalf of the University; his conception of its purpose; the chief provisions of the charter.— The protest of the House of Assembly in 1828 against the charter; petition to the King.—Action of the House of Assembly and of the Legislative Council in regard to the charter, 1829.— Popular petition to the Imperial Parliament, 1830.— The Charter Amendment bills of 1835 and 1836; passed by House of Assembly, but rejected by Council; reasons given for this rejection.—Attitude of Imperial Government on the University question; report of a Committee of the House of Commons, 1828; instructions of Colonial office to Sir John Colborne, 1828; request for a surrender of the charter, 1831; refusal of the College Council and reasons therefor.— The Charter Amendment Act of 1837; its chief provisions.— A Presbyterian professorship of theology in King's College; suggested by Committee of Imperial House of Commons, 1828; agitated by United Presbytery of Upper Canada from 1831 onward; approved by Legislative Council, 1837.— Claims of Presbyterians ignored by King's College Council, 1837; appeal to the British Colonial Office; adverse report of the Educational Commission of 1839.—Act incorporating the Presbyterian University of Kingston, 1840; provision for the endowment of a Chair of Theology in the institution from King's College funds.— Name of the institution changed by Royal Charter in 1841 to Queen's College; no mention in the charter of a Chair of Theology, hence grant from King's College withheld.— The University Act of 1849 and the complete secularization of King's College; its name changed to the University of Toronto.

CHAPTER IX..Page 102
EDUCATIONAL TENDENCIES IN ONTARIO, 1846-1906

The Elementary Schools: Work of Dr. Ryerson; the School Act of 1871; appointment of a Minister of Education, 1876; Dr. J. H. Sangster's description of the public schools of 1850; forces which wrought a change for the better.— Detailed character of the present School Law.

Secondary Schools: The District Grammar School of 1850.— Reforms of 1853.— Changes made by School Act of 1871.— Subsequent changes.— Present high school conditions.

Normal and Model Schools: Dr. Ryerson's visit to Europe and the United States.— Founding of the Provincial Normal School at Toronto.— Opposition to the Normal School idea.— Normal School course made purely professional in 1871.— Other Normal Schools established.— Common characteristics of these schools.— The Ontario Normal College.— Recently established Faculty of Education in the University of Toronto.— Early model schools; their defects.— Reforms of 1871.— Recent changes.

The Provincial University: Two chief lines of progress.— The movement towards centralization.— University Federation movement, 1853-1901.— Principles underlying present federation.— Institutions outside of federation.—Conclusion,—endowments and appropriations represented by the University of Toronto as at present constituted.

INTRODUCTORY NOTE.

The period with which the following study mainly deals is not one arbitrarily selected. It possesses characteristics which distinguish it from the years which preceded it and those which followed. The year 1791, following close upon the first English settlement, marked the creation of the province of Upper Canada by the Constitutional Act, while in 1841 came into effect the Act of Union which again joined Upper to Lower Canada; but these provinces were again separated twenty-five years later by the Confederation Act which made the Dominion of the present day.

The half-century from 1791 onward was one of marked growth in the population and material wealth of the Province, but, more important for the purpose of the present study, it witnessed also the development of certain religious, political and social ideals. It was a time of ferment and of struggle and it did not pass without the shedding of patriot blood, but through the dissension and the turmoil there were established three things which are the finest fruit of the thousand years or more of Anglo-Saxon civilization—responsible government, religious equality and the free school. Moreover, free public education was made possible only through the overthrow of autocracy in church and state; hence no apology is needed for the frequent reference in the following pages to incidents which might seem at the first glance to be purely political or religious in their character.

The debt of the writer to one predecessor in the field is manifest throughout. Dr. Hodgins in his *Documentary History of Education in Upper Canada* has compiled from an immense number of sources, many of which are not readily available, a mass of information, the value of which to the student of educational conditions in Ontario can scarcely be overestimated. In a Documentary History, however, very little beyond a chronological arrangement can be attempted and completeness must be secured even at the apparent sacrifice at times of relevancy.

The present study while in a measure chronological and descriptive, aims to be selective and interpretative as well. In its selective character it may be regarded as supplementing the work just referred to, while from the interpretative side it may furnish an element which seems to be lacking in such an otherwise excellent work as Dr. Ross's *School System of Ontario*. The supplementary chapter, it may be remarked, is added with a view to throwing some light on the chapters which precede it by furnishing to the reader a summary of educational events subsequent to 1841. It must not be regarded as an attempt to recount adequately the educational history of the Province from 1841 till the present day.

CHAPTER I.

THE POLITICAL AND SOCIAL BACKGROUND.

The purpose of this chapter is not to attempt a complete résumé of the political and social life of Upper Canada during the period indicated; such would be in itself an undertaking of greater magnitude than the entire present work professes to be. Its design is rather to call the attention of the reader to certain salient facts without a knowledge of which any clear understanding of the educational situation would be impossible.

A brief sketch of the conditions which preceded the first extensive emigration to the territory known for many years as Upper Canada and now known as the Province of Ontario, forms a fitting preface to the story of the later period.

During the period of French occupation,—the *Ancien Régime*, so-called,—there were several fortified posts, partly for military, partly for trading purposes, along the great stretch of waterway which now forms part of the boundary between Canada and the United States. Three of these were: Fort Cataraqui, near where the city of Kingston now stands; Fort Rouillé, on the site of the present city of Toronto, and Fort Niagara, on the river of that name. Two of these posts—the first and the last-named—were continued when the English succeeded the French as masters of the soil, and thus naturally they became centres for the distribution of the settlers who came into Upper Canada in such large numbers in the years immediately following the war of the American Revolution. Previous to this time the French had made little attempt at colonization in Upper Canada. Naturally there had been a certain extension of settlement westward from Montreal, along the St. Lawrence and Ottawa rivers. Then again a few of the French families who clustered about the trading post at Detroit had crossed the Detroit River and settled in what is now Canadian territory. Of these early settlers, the present French-speaking inhabitants of the County of Essex are, in the main, the descendants. This emigration was, however, so insignificant from a numerical standpoint, that it can safely be said that in 1783 (the date of the close of the

Revolutionary War), the entire Province was practically untouched by civilization.

The nearness of this virgin territory coupled with the active encouragement given by the British Government resulted in the transplanting, in the years between 1784 and 1800, of large bodies of Loyalist settlers from the United States. The story of the persecutions which hastened this emigration does not properly belong to this narrative, and has, moreover, been told in detail by other writers. We are concerned here wholly with that part of the history of the settlement of Upper Canada which will help us to a better understanding of subsequent educational conditions in the Province.

The Loyalists in question were of English, Dutch and German blood, and came almost wholly from New York, Pennsylvania, New Jersey and the New England States. They were able to bring very little money or moveable property with them; hence, for some years, they were dependent to a considerable degree upon the bounty of the British Government. Liberal grants of land ranging, according to circumstances, from two hundred to two thousand acres were made to them; free rations were dealt out, though at irregular intervals; and seed grain and farm implements were distributed to assist them to become self-supporting as speedily as possible. All this mitigated, though it by no means wholly removed, the hardships of their lot. The chief Loyalist settlements were along the Upper St. Lawrence, on the Bay of Quinte (near the eastern end of Lake Ontario), in the Niagara peninsula and westward along the northeastern shore of Lake Erie. Because of the industry and thrift of their inhabitants, these districts soon came to rank among the most prosperous portions of the Province. Closely akin in character to these first settlers were the various bodies of Quakers, Dutch and Pennsylvania Germans, who came into Upper Canada during the first quarter of the nineteenth century. In fact there was a marked emigration from the United States throughout the greater part of this period in spite of the fact that from 1812 till 1815 Great Britain and the United States were at war.

The European immigrants to Upper Canada were almost wholly from the British Isles. Indeed, the only continental element

Political and Social Background.

in the population of the Province during the fifty years of which we are speaking, if we exclude a band of Germans who emigrated to Markham Township in 1794 after a brief stay in New York State, seems to have been contributed by a few French Royalists, Swiss and Alsatians.[1] The vanguard from Great Britain were bands of Scotch Highlanders who settled in the County of Glengarry in the closing years of the eighteenth and the opening years of the nineteenth century.

A noticeable feature of the disposal of the British emigrants was their settlement on large blocks of land consisting of a township or more. So clearly were the distinctions of race and religion marked by geographical position that even to-day one can find a township which is predominantly Highland Scotch, another which is almost wholly Lowland Scotch in character, others whose very names signify that the ancestors of many of the present inhabitants came, as the case may be, from the north of Ireland, from the south of Ireland, from Devonshire, Cornwall or from the German counties of Pennsylvania. In distinct contrast with the policy of settlement by townships, was that of Colonel Talbot the owner by Royal Grant of an immense tract of land in the western portion of the Province. He very wisely distributed his settlers after "the checkerboard fashion" so that no two families of the same nationality were placed side by side. The general policy of assigning land, to which we have just referred, joined with other factors which will presently be mentioned, tended to hinder any concerted action by the inhabitants of the Province in asserting their political rights and hence helped materially in continuing a governmental policy under which the rights of the average citizen, as regarded from a more modern view-point, received very scant consideration indeed.

Another fact which is worthy of notice in this connection was the autocratic behavior of the administration in regard to the granting of land. Mr. Robert Thorpe, one of the Provincial judges in 1807, in referring to the "shop-keeper aristocracy" which surrounded the Lieutenant-Governor and influenced his official conduct, says: "Next to themselves, their families and friends, they give unbounded tracts of land in the finest situa-

---

[1] See "Ethnographical Elements of Ontario" in *Papers and Records of the Ont. Hist. Soc.*, Vol. III, 1901.

tions, at whatever rules or fees they choose and then barter this land to our greatest enemies in the States; next they keep from the House of Assembly all accounts of the greatest part of the public money, thus denying them the first privilege given by the British Act of Parliament which established their Constitution."[1] Mr. Robert Gourlay, an intelligent and patriotic Scotchman who came to Upper Canada in 1817, and who made a thorough investigation of the resources of the Province with a view to "a grand system of emigration," speaks of "the mean, selfish, unprincipled and unfeeling conduct of the Provincial Government in regard to the granting of land."[2] British emigrants, according to his statement, had to "dance attendance for weeks and months together before they could get a hearing from the Land Granting Department and when at last they were heard they were sent twenty or thirty miles into the wilderness where even native Americans could scarcely exist."[3] All this of course tended not only to retard the development of the Province, but also to increase greatly the popular bitterness against the powerful clique who thus sacrificed the general welfare to their own private convenience and emolument.

If this were a history of the Province as a whole rather than an attempt to describe a particular phase of its political and social life, we might go on to speak here of various other arbitrary acts of the Executive which further estranged the popular regard and which eventually led to an armed uprising (the Mackenzie Rebellion of 1837) on the part of a radical wing of the popular party. A few of these acts will be mentioned later in connection with certain specific phases of the general subject under consideration. For a statement of the remainder the reader is referred to any one of the Histories of Canada, mentioned in the bibliography at the close of this work.

A brief explanation of the structure of the Provincial Government will here be in order. Canada was at the time a Crown Colony, that is, its more important affairs were administered by the British Government or by officials appointed by that government. The highest representative of the Crown was the Governor-General who resided at Quebec. The immediate execu-

---

[1] Letter to Sir George Shee. *Canadian Archives*, Series Q, Vol. 305, p. 189, quoted in full in *Report of Dom. Archivist for 1892–93*, note D. p. 57.
[2] *A Statistical Account of Upper Canada*, Vol. II, p. 418.
[3] *Ibid*, p. 420.

tive authority in Upper Canada was in the hands of a Lieutenant-Governor whose headquarters were at the Provincial Capital, York (later Toronto). The immediate advisers of the Lieutenant-Governor were known as the Executive Council. They were appointed by him and most of them held important and lucrative positions under the Government. The legislative functions were in the hands of (1) a Legislative Council, also appointed by the Lieutenant-Governor, and from which the Executive Council was frequently recruited; (2) a House of Assembly, the members of which were chosen every few years by the qualified voters of the Province.

It can be easily seen from the foregoing that the part actually taken by the people in the management of their affairs was a very modest one and indeed might practically be said to disappear under an Executive wedded to aristocratic ideals. That the Executive was at times of the character just mentioned is very clearly shown by the following statement of Lieutenant-Governor Sir Francis Gore in justification of the dismissal of Judge Robert Thorpe from the bench for political activity obnoxious to the administration. "I cannot help entertaining the hope," remarks Sir Francis, "that the measure which has been adopted, however painful, will have the most salutary influence in preventing the further progress of that spirit of equality and want of subordination which too much prevails among the lower ranks of this Province."[1]

In fact throughout this whole period the House of Assembly, in so far as it kept itself free from the dictation of the Executive, served two main purposes, neither of which was strictly legislative in character. (1) Through its investigations, reports and debates, it made the real needs of the Province apparent to the people at large and thus performed an educative function. (2) Through petitions which, from time to time, it laid at the foot of the Throne, it called the attention of the British Government to the crying abuses which existed in the Province and thus helped indirectly to check the autocratic tendencies of the Lieutenant-Governors and their advisers. Through these petitions also it helped to create, in the mother country, a sentiment which made possible the establishment, in 1841, of the

[1] Letter to Lord Castlereagh, in *Canadian Archives*, Series Q, Vol. 310, p. 15, quoted in *Report of Dom. Archivist for 1892-93*, note D, p. 87.

principle that the members of the Executive and Legislative Councils should be men who possessed the confidence of the people as a whole.

A brief statement of the municipal organization of the Province is also necessary. Before the creation of the Province of Upper Canada, by the Constitutional Act of 1791, that portion of Canada had been divided into four districts, viz.: Lunenburgh, Mecklenburgh, Nassau and Hesse. The first Parliament of Upper Canada, in 1792, re-named them the Eastern, Midland, Home and Western Districts. The Parliament of 1798 established eight districts which were subdivided into twenty-three counties, and these in turn into one hundred and fifty-eight townships.[1] The names of these various districts will appear more than once in the following chapters, hence, they need not be given here. Throughout the whole of our period, the district and the township (with its included school districts) formed the units of school administration. At a later date the district was abandoned and its function, so far at least as the control of the schools was concerned, transferred to the county.

The various religious denominations of the time naturally exerted a considerable influence on the educational history of the Province. Of these denominations, in their more general aspects we will now briefly speak, leaving for a subsequent chapter the consideration in detail of the relationship of certain of them to the public schools.

The facts, numerical and otherwise, in regard to the religious condition of the Province in 1792, are thus set forth in an official report made in that year to Lieutenant-Governor John Graves Simcoe. "Of this (the Anglican) Church" remarks the author of the report, "I am myself a member and am sorry to say that the state of it in this Province is not very flattering. A very small proportion of the inhabitants of Upper Canada have been educated in this persuasion and the emigrants to be expected from the United States will be for the most part Sectaries or Dissenters and nothing prevents the teachers of this class from being proportionately numerous but the inability of the people at present to provide for their support. In the Eastern District, the most populous part of the Province, there is

---

[1] Gourlay, *A Statistical Account of Upper Canada*, Vol. I, pp. 116–120.

no Church clergyman. They have a Presbyterian minister, formerly Chaplain to the 84th Regiment, who receives from the Government £50 p. ann. They have also a Lutheran minister who is supported by his congregation and the Roman Catholic priest settled at St. Regis occasionally officiates for the Scotch Highlanders settled in the lower part of the district who are very numerous and all Catholics. There are also many Dutch colonists in this part of the Province who have made several attempts to get a teacher of their own sect, but hitherto without success."

" In the Midland District where the members of the Church are more numerous than in any other part of the Province, there are two Church clergymen who are allowed £100 stg. p. ann. each by the Government and £50 by the Society for the Propagation of the Gospel. There are also here some itinerant Methodist preachers the followers of whom are numerous and many of the inhabitants of the greatest property are Dutch colonists who have for some time past been using their endeavors to get a minister of their own sect among them. In the Home District there is one clergyman who has been settled here since the month of July last. The Scots Presbyterians who are pretty numerous here and to which sect the most respectable part of the inhabitants belong, have built a meeting-house and raised a subscription for a minister of their own who is shortly expected among them. There are here also many Methodists and Dutch Calvinists."

" In the Western District there are no other clergymen than those of the Church of Rome. The Protestant inhabitants here are principally Presbyterians."[1]

The relative standing of the various denominations as regards numbers seems to have been practically the same some thirty years later, for in Mr. Gourlay's " Statistical Account," published in 1822, we find the following,—" In Upper Canada there are six ministers of the Church of England residing at Cornwall, Kingston, Ernestown and Fredericksburg. They solemnize marriages but there is no ecclesiastical court. Dissenters of all denominations are tolerated and protected by law. They are not subject to tithes or civil disabilities nor disqualified for

---

Report of Richard Cartwright Jun'r, 1702. on "The Marriage Law in Upper Canada In *Report of Dominion Archivist for* 1891, Note I, pp. 85-86.

office or a seat in the Legislature. Their contracts respecting the support of public worship are legally enforceable. Ordained ministers of the Scotch, Lutheran and Calvinist churches upon producing satisfactory credentials in a Court of Sessions are authorized to perform marriages where one of the parties to be married is a member of their respective societies. Any denomination holding the distinguishing Calvinistic doctrines is included under the term Calvinist, as such, Presbyterian, Congregational and Baptist clergymen exercise the power of marriage. The dissenting denominations are Presbyterian, Lutheran, Methodists, Congregationalists, Moravians, Anabaptists, Roman Catholics, Quakers, Menonists and Tunkers. Several of them are more numerous than the Episcopalians. The most numerous of all are the Methodists who are spread over the whole Province. Next in number are the Presbyterians who are of the Dutch Reformed church, the Church of Scotland and Scotch seceders or the Associate Reformed Synod. The Presbyterians appear to be increasing in numbers and respectability."

"The Roman Catholics, who are comparatively few, are attached to the government and grateful for the religious freedom which they enjoy and by which they are distinguished from their brethren in Ireland."

"Quakers, Menonists and Tunkers, being conscientiously scrupulous of bearing arms are conditionally exempt from military duties."[1]

Some ten years later (in 1831) the Lieutenant-Governor, Sir John Colborne, thus describes the "Ecclesiastical Establishments" of the Province in a letter to Lord Goderich, the secretary of state for the colonies: "There are thirty-seven missionary establishments (of the Church of England) under the direction of the Bishop of Quebec assisted by two archdeacons. . . . The Roman Catholic are under the control of Bishop Macdonnell who was last year appointed Bishop of Regiopolis (i. e., Kingston). The Presbyterians in communion with the Church of Scotland have about twenty ministers officiating in churches established in various parts of the Province. There are also about eighteen congregations unconnected with the

---

[1] *Op. cit.*, Vol. I, pp. 233–234.

Church of Scotland. . . . The Episcopal Methodists under the direction of the Canadian Conference have about sixty preachers and it is said about forty thousand communicants."

" By returns received in April last, the population of the Province amounted to about 234,000 being an increase since 1829 of 38,632."[1]

Making all allowance for inaccuracies in the foregoing due to prejudice or misinformation, it is manifest that the dissenting denominations were greatly in the majority. In spite of this fact, however, the Reverend Doctor Strachan, the leader of the Anglican church in the Province and its representative in the Legislative and Executive Councils, resolutely and persistently claimed for that body all the privileges of the Establishment in England. This of course included the sole right of the Church to the enjoyment of the clergy reserves (an immense tract of land set apart by the Constitutional Act of 1791 for the support of " a Protestant clergy ") and to the control of public education in all its departments.

Naturally the so-called dissenters withstood these claims as unjust to themselves and to the important work which they were doing and as inconsistent with the spirit of the new country. They united in opposing the claims of the Church of England to a monopoly of the clergy reserves, but differed among themselves as to the disposal which should be made of the lands in question. The Church of Scotland, for example, and a branch of the Methodists (the British Wesleyans) favored a partition of these lands among the various Protestant denominations. The Canadian Methodists, on the contrary, through their official organ, the *Christian Guardian,* and its able editor, the Reverend Egerton Ryerson, strenuously advocated the devotion of the reserves to the support of public schools. Mr. Ryerson's position is thus stated in an editorial which appeared in the journal just mentioned, in 1838: " In respect to the ecclesiastical affairs of this province, I still adhere to the principles and views with which I set out in 1826. I believe the endowment of the priesthood of any church in this province will be an evil to that church, as well as impolitic in the gov-

---

[1] Letter to Lord Goderich, in *Canadian Archives*, Series Q, Vol. 357-2, p. 282, quoted in *Report of Dom. Archivist for* 1899–1900, Note C, pp. 68–72.

ernment. In accordance with the declaration put forth by several principal ministers in the Methodist Church in January last, I believe that the appropriation of the proceeds of the clergy reserves to general educational purposes will be the most satisfactory disposal of them that can be made."[1]

Another cause for complaint and opposition was the special rights which the clergy of the Church of England enjoyed in regard to the solemnization of marriage. The "Calvinistic" clergy, as we have seen, might exercise this right under certain restrictions. To the Methodist clergy as being Arminian rather than Calvinist, it was wholly denied. Not only was this felt to be a hardship by the Methodists; it was regarded as an indignity as well.[2]

All this will help us to appreciate the fact that religious and political questions became inextricably involved at times, since religious disabilities could be removed only through an agitation which was more or less political in its character. These semi-political, semi-religious controversies frequently had an educational bearing and thus served to complicate educational issues. To a discussion of this phase of the subject one or more chapters will later be devoted, hence we may now pass to a consideration of other topics.

Of the general conditions of life during the period little perhaps need be said. They were such as pioneer communities invariably have to encounter. Traveling, except by water, was slow and difficult. Often settlers took up farms in "the bush" before roads were built. One of the regulations enforced by Colonel Talbot in the Talbot settlement was that each settler should make at least a quarter of a mile of public road. The Canada Land Company in the opening of "the Huron Tract" for settlement exercised still greater foresight. Roads and bridges were built and town sites planned before any settlers were introduced. Such cases as the two just mentioned were, however, decidedly exceptional. Another feature which greatly hindered proper means of communication and transportation was the existence of large blocks of unoccupied land, such as the clergy reserves, which interposed barriers of unbroken forest

---

[1] Quoted in *Biography of Ryerson* by Nathaniel Burwash, p. 115.
[2] The disabilities here mentioned were removed by the so-called Imperial Marriage Act of 1832.

between various of the occupied portions of the Province. Of the stage-coaches of the time, Dr. Scadding in his *Toronto of Old* says: " We are informed by a contemporary advertisement now before us, that ' on the 20th of September next (1816), a stage will commence running between York and Niagara; it will leave York every Monday and arrive at Niagara on Thursday; and leave Queenstown every Friday. Baggage is to be considered at the risk of the owner and the fare to be paid in advance.' "[1] Thus it will be seen that in 1816 it took four days to accomplish a journey which is now easily achieved by rail in as many hours. " In 1835," Dr. Scadding informs us, " Mr. William Weller was the proprietor of a line of stages between Toronto and Hamilton known as " The Telegraph Line " and " Engaged to take passengers through by daylight (a distance of some forty miles) on the Lake Road, during the winter season."[2] Of communication with the mother country in 1836, Mrs. Jameson, an authoress of the period, who resided in Toronto, has the following to say in her journal: " It is now seven weeks since the date of the last letters from my dear, far-distant home. . . . The archdeacon (Dr. Strachan) told me, by way of comfort, that when he came to settle in this country (in 1799), there was only one mail-post from England in the course of a whole year, and it was called, as if in mockery, the Express."[3]

Newspapers were few and, it would appear, short-lived as well. Mr. Lindsey in his *Life of William Lyon Mackenzie,* in discussing one of Mr. Mackenzie's newspaper-ventures (*The Colonial Advocate,* established at York in 1824), remarks: " It was doubtful whether any newspaper which had then been published in Upper Canada had repaid the proprietor the cost of its production. Any publisher who sent a thousand sheets through the post-office must pay $800 a year quarterly in advance."[4] Of post-office conditions in 1824, Mr. Lindsey informs us: " Though some of the other settlements were well supplied with post-offices, there were none at all on the southwestern frontier from Chippewa by Fort Erie to the mouth of the Grand River. The three thousand settlers in Dumfries and

[1] *Op. cit.,* p. 49.
[2] *Toronto of Old,* p. 49.
[3] Vol. I, p. 182, quoted by Dr. Scadding in the work just mentioned.
[4] *Op. cit.,* Vol. I, p. 36.

Waterloo had to travel from sixteen to forty miles before they reached a post-office. Postmasters received nothing for distributing newspapers and so were careless about their delivery. Other modes of distribution were occasionally resorted to by publishers to avoid the heavy postal-tax."[1]

Having thus briefly reviewed the chief features of the early political and social life of the Province, we may now proceed to a study of certain movements and institutions which, while the outcome of this wider life, were directly educational in character. We will consider first the various attempts made to provide for the support of public schools out of the public domain.

[1] *The Life and Times of William Lyon Mackenzie*, Vol. I, p. 64.

CHAPTER II.

THE LAND GRANTS FOR SCHOOLS.

The first Lieutenant-Governor of Upper Canada after the separation of that province from Lower Canada by the Constitutional Act of 1791, was Lieutenant-Colonel John Graves Simcoe, an ex-officer of the British forces in the war of the American Revolution and an ex-member of the British Parliament. As governor he actively encouraged the settlement of United Empire Loyalists in Upper Canada and sought in various other ways to promote the growth of the infant province. Being deeply chagrined at the success of the revolted colonies, he was naturally most anxious to develop in Upper Canada a sentiment of loyalty towards the political and religious institutions of the mother country. The means which, in his mind, would best conduce to this end were the appointment of an ecclesiastical official charged with the superintendence of the missionary enterprises of the Church of England in the Province, and the establishment of a provincial university. This university was to be—to use his own language—"A scion of the respectable stock of Oxford and Cambridge."[1]

The following extracts from letters written by Governor Simcoe during his stay in Canada (1792-1796) will illustrate what has just been said and will give some further insight into the motives which actuated his official conduct. In a letter written in 1791 to Sir Joseph Banks, President of the Royal Society, he says, "In a literary way I should be glad to lay the foundation stone of some society that I trust might hereafter conduce to the extension of science. Schools have been shamefully neglected—a college of a higher class would be eminently useful, and would give a tone of principle and manners that would be of infinite support to government."[2] He returns to the same theme in a letter written in the following year to the Right Honorable Henry Dundas, Secretary of State. "But the question of higher education is of still more importance; (i. e. than

---
[1] From a letter to the first Church of England Bishop of Quebec, quoted in *Doc. Hist.*, Vol. I, p. 13.
[2] *Doc. Hist.*, Vol. I, p. 11.

certain other matters to which he had just referred) lower education, being less expensive, may in the meantime, be provided by relations, and more remotely by school lands. The higher must be indebted to the liberality of the British Government, as, owing to the cheapness of education in the United States, the gentlemen of Upper Canada will send their children there, which would tend to pervert their British principles."[1]

The enthusiasm of Governor Simcoe for higher education did not meet, however, with a very sympathetic response from the officials of the Home Government. Secretary Dundas, in a reply to the letter from which we have just quoted, says, "As to schools and a university, I think that the schools will be sufficient for some time."[2] Much more outspoken still in his lack of sympathy is the Duke of Portland, Secretary of State, who remarks in a letter dated June 22, 1796: "As the want of schoolmasters is particularly noticed in your letter to the bishop, I should be far from unwilling to recommend that some provision should be made here for their maintenance; but in doing this I must observe that my ideas of schoolmasters best suited to the present state of Upper Canada are such as are thoroughly competent to teach reading, writing, accounts and mensuration."[3]

The apathy of the Home Government did not, however, prevent Governor Simcoe from making an earnest effort to secure an appropriation from the public domain for the needs of a university when that institution should be established. Witness the following paragraph from a letter written to the Duke of Portland a few days after the receipt of the communication from which we have just quoted. " In the meantime the sevenths of the Crown will become gradually productive as lands which have been granted shall be cultivated, or withdrawn from the market, and appropriations may be made agreeably to the opinion of the Council, to be sold hereafter for public purposes, the first and chief of which I beg to offer with all respect and deference, to your grace, must be the erection and endowment of a university from which more than any other source or circumstance whatever, a grateful attachment to His Majesty,

---
[1] *Doc. Hist.*, Vol. I, p. 11.
[2] *Ibid.*
[3] *Ibid*, p. 14.

morality and religion will be fostered and take root throughout the whole Province."

The Reverend Doctor Ryerson, in his *History of the United Empire Loyalists,* refers to Governor Simcoe as "the father of constitutional, pure and progressive government in Upper Canada."[1] However true this statement may be as applied to other phases of his activity, the term "progressive" can apply only with serious limitations to his educational policy. His ideal in this regard was a reproduction, in their essential characteristics, of the English public schools and universities. Elementary education was to him, as to most Englishmen of his day, a matter for charity or private enterprise. He failed to apprehend the fact that among the settlers of this new country there existed a popular attitude which would in the next quarter century become increasingly hostile to aristocratic ideals in education and to sectarian domination in the public schools. Statesmanlike he was, however, in his emphasis on the desirability of early setting apart a portion of the public land for educational purposes, though he failed to foresee that public endowment would eventually lead to public control and to a democratic and a non-denominational, if not a purely secular, system of schools.

Governor Simcoe was recalled in 1796 but his appeals had evidently produced some effect since in the following year (1797) the acting-governor—the Honorable Peter Russell—received from the Duke of Portland a communication announcing on behalf of the King "His (Majesty's) most gracious intention to comply with the legislature of his Province of Upper Canada in such manner as shall be judged most effectual, first, by the establishment of free grammar schools in those districts in which they are called for, and in the process of time by establishing other seminaries of a larger and more comprehensive nature for the promotion of religious and moral learning, and the study of the arts and sciences. With this view the President is directed to consult the members of His Majesty's Executive Council, and the Judges and Law Officers of the Crown in Upper Canada, and to report to the Secretary of State in which manner, and to what extent, a portion of the Crown Lands

---

[1] *History of the U. E. Loyalists,* p. 312.

may be appropriated and rendered productive towards the formation of a fund for the above purpose."[1] The committee was appointed as directed and its report submitted in the following year. This report is too lengthy to be given in detail, but five of its recommendations are of sufficient importance to be quoted here:

(1) That an appropriation of 500,000 acres . . . will form a sufficient fund for the establishment and maintenance of the royal foundation of four grammar schools and an university in the Province of Upper Canada.

(2) That the present circumstances of the Province call for the erection of two of these schools, one at the town of Kingston and the other at the town of Newark (Niagara).

(3) That for the purpose of building a plain but solid and substantial house, containing a school room sufficient to contain one hundred boys, and apartments for the master large enough for the accommodation of a moderate family and the reception of from ten to twelve boys as boarders, the sum of £3000 provincial currency for each will be a sufficient allowance.

(4) That for the purpose of raising that sum a portion of the appropriated tract be sold in the manner directed by His Grace the Duke of Portland with respect to the other waste lands of the Crown.

(5) That for the purpose of defraying the salaries of a master and undermaster, in case an undermaster should be thought necessary, and also for the purpose of keeping the buildings in repair and making such additions thereto as circumstances shall require, the annual sum of £180 provisional currency for each school is a sufficient allowance.[2]

In spite of the fact, which is abundantly proven in the foregoing quotations, that in the correspondence and deliberations concerning the Royal Grant of 1797, grammar schools were regarded as having the prior claim, the university or, as it was called, King's College, was made, throughout the whole period with which we have to deal, the chief, and in fact almost the sole beneficiary.

This circumstance can, to a great extent, be attributed to the influence of one man—the Reverend John Strachan. This gentleman came to Upper Canada from Scotland in 1799 with the expectation of becoming the head of the projected university. Since there was no immediate prospect of the university being established, he accepted a position as tutor in the family of the Honorable Richard Cartwright of Kingston. Subsequently he

---
[1] *Doc. Hist.*, Vol. I, p. 18.
[2] *Ibid.* Vol. I, p. 23.

became clergyman of the Church of England, master of the grammar school at Cornwall and master of the Home District grammar school at York. He came to occupy at a later period many important offices. In the Church, he was made archdeacon of York and eventually bishop of Toronto. In the field of education, he was head of the General Board of Education during the ten years of its existence (1823-1833) and President of King's College from its inception till 1849. In that year he resigned the presidency because of the secularization of the college through a radical change in the nature of its charter, and devoted his energies to the building up of a rival institution under the auspices of the Church of England and known as Trinity College. As a member of the Legislative Council for many years and also of the Executive Council of the Lieutenant-Governor, he exerted great political influence. He was naturally from the first a zealous champion of the cause of the university and had much to do with the keeping of the needs of higher education prominently before the Legislature and the people. His official position, united with a strong personality, a broad scholarship and a high personal character made him a commanding figure in the educational life of the province for nearly half a century.

It will be in order now to review briefly the various appropriations of land for educational purposes made during the fifty years subsequent to 1797.

The undesirability of an immediate sale of the half million or more of acres at the disposal of the Provincial Government for school purposes is illustrated by the fact, that 81,000 acres of land, sold in 1800 to defray the expense of building a public road, realized only £411, 16s. and the further fact that when the executive desired to secure a house and four acres of land at Niagara to be used for grammar school purposes, the owner of the property asked in exchange 73,000 acres of public land. The chief reason for the failure of the negotiations seems to have been not any belief on the part of the prospective purchasers that the owner's terms were exorbitant but the discovery that the house in question was within easy range of the guns of the American fort across the river.

Apart from the foregoing, no formal action looking to the disposal of any portion of the land grant for schools seems to have been taken before 1819. In that year, the Executive Council urged the Lieutenant-Governor, Sir Peregrine Maitland, to secure "a formal sanction under the Royal Sign Manual or the signature of His Majesty's principal Secretary of State for the Colonies, to sell, lease, grant and dispose of the said 500,000 acres of land, for the purpose of establishing a university in this province." A sufficient reason for excluding the grammar schools from participation in this grant existed, in their opinion, in the fact "that provision for district schools is not now required out of this fund, being (already) made by the Legislature (by the Act of 1807)."[1]

This recommendation was never carried out, though, some ten years later, an endowment almost equal in value to that suggested by the Executive Council was assigned to the university. "According to the Deed of Endowment of the 3rd of January 1828, the quantity of land conveyed to the university from the Crown Reserves was 225,944 acres. . . . The Crown Reserves thus converted into University Endowment consisted of lands situate in various parts of Upper Canada in actual or nominal occupation, under lease, at rate of rental fixed by a certain scale established by the Provincial Government, and a large proportion of the lots were in an improved or cultivated state."[2] This involved a resumption on the part of the Crown of an equal amount of land from the original grant. The reason for this exchange is given in some detail by Dr. Strachan in his address at the opening of King's College in 1842. "From the first settlement of the Province, two-sevenths of the land in the settled Townships had been reserved—one for the maintenance of the Protestant Clergy, called Clergy Reserves—the other still remained for special purposes at the disposal of the Government, and were called Crown Reserves. These latter being still in the Crown, had become in many places very valuable, from the settlements around them, and if brought into the market would command reasonable prices much more than the lands which had been originally appropriated for the district

---

[1] *Doc. Hist.*, Vol. I, p. 151.
[2] From Report of Commissioners appointed by Lord Elgin, Governor-General, in 1848 to enquire into the affairs of King's College, pp. 16 and 17, quoted in *Doc. Hist.*, Vol. I, p. 205.

(grammar) schools and university, which had been carelessly selected and continued, from their remoteness, almost unsaleable. Now, to secure a complete endowment for a university it was submitted by Sir Peregrine Maitland to His Majesty's Government to exchange a portion of the school lands for a like quantity of the Crown Reserves. For the mere purpose of granting lots to settlers, the school lands were as useful to the Government as the Crown Reserves; but such an exchange, if it could be effected, would place at His Excellency's disposal an endowment which might be made almost immediately available."[1]

Under the much more favorable conditions thus brought about the financial standing of the university steadily improved, so that in January, 1839, it was estimated that up to that date there had been sold 93,737¾ acres at an aggregate price of £55,224, 14s., 7d. In addition to the revenue derived from the investment of this sum, the income from leased lands must be taken into consideration. In February, 1842, this was stated as being £1862 per annum, with arrears of rent amounting to £15,515, 5s., 9d., of which £10,000 might be recovered in six years.[2] Thus, when, in 1842, the university began its work as a teaching body, it had available sources of income which, for that time, were quite considerable.

Closely connected with the grants and expenditures for university purposes was the attempted endowment in 1820, from university funds, of a "National" system of schools patterned after the system of the same name in England, and the assignment of 66,000 acres of the school lands to Upper Canada College, "the superior grammar school" founded in 1829 by Lieutenant-Governor Sir John Colborne. Since both of these institutions will be treated at some length in subsequent chapters, no further reference to them is here necessary.

In marked contrast with the attitude of the Executive Council of 1819, a select committee of the House of Assembly on Education advocated, in 1831, the use of the land grant chiefly, if not solely, for grammar and common school purposes. After reviewing briefly the educational proceedings of 1797, 1798 and

---

[1] Pp. 36–38 of address. Quoted in *Doc. Hist.*, Vol. I, p. 204.
[2] From a statement of the finances of King's College appended to the *Journals of the House of Assembly* for 1839. Quoted in *Doc. Hist.*, Vol. III, p. 182.

1819, the committee express the opinion that the "original intention of the Legislature of 1797 has been lost sight of and for no other reason that your committee can discover than that a grammar school has by Act of the Legislature (in 1807) been already established in each district with a salary of £100 to the master."[1]

The recommendations of the committee with the data therefor are summed up in the following paragraph:

The whole reservation of 549,217 acres if sold at the average price of ten shillings ($2) per acre would give a capital of £274,608, producing, if invested at the rate of 5 per cent. interest, an annual income of £13,730 a sum sufficient to endow the schools (as detailed in the following table) which your Committee conceive to be necessary besides leaving an important balance to defray the expense of the sales and the collecting of the money.

11 (Free) grammar schools at £400 each is....	£4,400
1 College at York	2,000
132 Township (Common) Schools being 12 in each District at £50.....................	6,600
Balance to defray the expense of sales, etc......	730
	£13,700 : $54,920[2]

The allusion to a "College at York" instead of a formal mention of King's College, for which a royal charter had been obtained four years previously, is significant as reflecting the hostile attitude of the House towards that institution on account of the sectarian character of the charter in question. In fact the House had, in 1829, gone so far as to pass a bill enlarging Upper Canada College into an undenominational university, hoping thereby to make the establishment of King's College unnecessary. Of course the real purport of the bill was easily detected by the Legislative Council who, accordingly, promptly rejected it.

There is little doubt that the House in its attacks on the management of the school lands and in its estimate of the immediate value of those lands, did not fully appreciate the practical difficulties of the situation. This fact is clearly shown in a report made in this same year to the Lieutenant-Governor by the Executive Council on the question of the

[1] *Doc. Hist.*, Vol. II, p. 22.
[2] *Ibid*, pp. 22–23.

endowment of the grammar schools with land. After making certain recommendations pointing to the gradual realization of a money endowment for the purpose mentioned, the report goes on to state:

> Before closing this report, the Executive Council think it proper to advert to the assertion frequently brought forward, that the School Reservation might have been made long ago far more productive and yielding by this time a large disposal fund.
>
> That so long as millions of acres were in course of grant (which was the case till 1828) by the Crown in fee simple, for almost nothing, and more than half the population were entitled, from various causes, to gratuitous grants, no lands could have been sold for any price near their value.
>
> Any objection, therefore, on this head is evidently founded in error; and calculations founded upon the receipt of large sums of money from sales which could never have been effected, can only be brought forward by those who have not fully understood the subject.[1]

Though all the parties concerned had by this time come to realize the justice of the claims of the grammar schools to a participation in the school lands, nothing in the way of positive legislation was accomplished till 1839 when by an Act of that year, 250,000 acres were definitely set apart for grammar school purposes. That this source of revenue was promptly utilized is proven by the fact that by the beginning of 1841 the amount invested in Provincial debentures on behalf of the grammar schools by the Council of King's College (the custodian of the fund) was nearly fifteen thousand pounds.[2]

When we turn to the common schools, we find that their claim to a share in the public domain was even more tardily acknowledged. As early as 1816 the House of Assembly and the Legislative Council united in an address to the Lieutenant-Governor asking for an appropriation of a part of the waste lands of the Crown for common school purposes. Though the Lieutenant-Governor in response assured the two houses of his sympathy with the movement, no further action seems to have been taken at that time. In December, 1831, there was presented to the House of Assembly a petition from certain inhabitants of the county of Oxford " praying that the House will address His Majesty praying him to authorize the Parlia-

---

[1] *Doc. Hist.*, Vol. II, p. 46.
[2] From Financial statement of the Bursar of King's College submitted at a meeting of the College Council, June 30th, 1841. In *Doc. Hist.*, Vol. IV, p. 62.

ment of this Province to appropriate — acres of the waste lands of the Crown to constitute a fund for the support of common schools."[1]

The committee to whom this address was referred recommended a grant, for the purpose mentioned, of one million acres. In addition they submitted a carefully wrought scheme whereby, in their opinion, a common school fund might be immediately created. This scheme involved, among other things, the use of the Provincial credit in the floating of a loan, this loan to be gradually repaid as the school lands came into the market. Nothing definite, however, came of this report, so a similar committee in the following year made a like recommendation. The reasons for their action are expressed with considerable force and concreteness. "Your committee," they declare, "feel it to be their duty, most earnestly and anxiously to draw the attention of your Honourable House to the astounding fact, that less is granted by the Provincial Legislature for educating the youth of three hundred thousand people than is required to defray the contingent expenses of one session of Parliament."

"How, indeed," they ask, "can useful improvements be promoted—the resources of the Province developed—its wealth increased—or its character elevated, if we continue to keep back the blessings of knowledge, and neglect to foster sound learning and scientific attainment?"[2]

The slowness of the Province in this regard is illustrated both in this report and the one of the preceding year by references to the endowment of common schools in various states of the Union—in New York State in particular.

The Select Committee of the House on Education in 1833 repeated the recommendations of its two immediate predecessors besides urging a material increase of the annual grant from the Provincial treasury for common school purposes. In the Speech from the Throne at the opening of the Parliamentary Session of 1835, the Lieutenant-Governor recommended "that township schools should be immediately organized and some practical mode decided on for applying the funds which should accrue from the sale of school lands not alienated by His Majesty's Government, and which had been placed under the

---

[1] *Doc. Hist.*, Vol. II, p. 49.
[2] Text of Committee's Report in *Doc. Hist.*, Vol. II, pp. 106–110.

Land Grants for Schools. 31

control of the Legislature, at the request of the House of Assembly, by the King."[1] This recommendation was, however, as barren of practical result as were those of the three committees of which mention has just been made. In the legislative session of 1839, a bill "to appropriate one million of acres of waste lands for the support of common schools in Upper Canada" was agreed upon by a joint committee of the House of Assembly and the Legislative Council and passed by the former body. Although not formally rejected by the Council, it was dropped in committee and so failed to become law.

It is very greatly to be regretted that through this action (or rather inaction) of the Legislative Council, a measure of so vital moment to the future welfare of the Province should have thus barely failed of success. Definite legislative action in the matter was thereby delayed for ten years. Moreover the land endowment eventually granted to the common schools of the Province was in consequence only one-half of what it might otherwise have been, since the grant of 1849 was made by the legislature of the united provinces and the million acres, at that time appropriated, divided equally between Upper and Lower Canada.

In thus reviewing the history of the land grant of 1797 and of the whole movement in Upper Canada for the endowment of public education from the public domain, one is strongly impressed with the influence exerted by the policy which was formulated by Governor Simcoe at the inception of the movement. The university, as has been shown, was given the first place, the grammar schools came second and the common schools last. That this attitude was opposed by a strong party in the House of Assembly and by a majority of the settlers of the province is doubtless true but popular sentiment could avail little against aristocratic prejudice entrenched behind an executive predisposed towards the conceptions of education then prevalent in the mother country, and inclined to look upon the movement for popular and non-denominational schools as an innovation tinged with disloyalty.

That this ultra-conservative attitude presented elements of incongruity even to visiting Englishmen, is illustrated by the

---
[1] *Doc. Hist.*, Vol. II, p. 161.

following extracts from *Three Years' Residence in Canada* by Mr. T. R. Preston, an English gentleman who spent the years 1837, 1838, and 1839 in the colony, and who, on his return to England, published the results of his observations. After reviewing in some detail educational proceedings from 1797 onward he says of the principle of a land endowment for public schools: " The method of its development (in Upper Canada) was replete with fallacy and injustice; attempting as it did to invert the legitimate order of a common inheritance. Though unquestionably an object most desirable per se, the establishment if it were possible of an institution in Upper Canada, conferring only on the few the higher grades of literary and scientific learning would be a strange burlesque, so long as elementary instruction remained in arrear of the general want."[1]

It must not be forgotten, moreover, that the bitter political struggles of the day introduced serious complications. They led to animosities of a personal character between members of the two branches of the Legislature and between members and factions of the House of Assembly itself. All this inevitably worked hardship to the cause of educational reform. When eventually, by the Act of Union of 1841 and by the proceedings which accompanied it, the principle of " responsible government " was established and the two legislative bodies brought more into harmony with each other, reforms which had been urged in vain for over thirty years were speedily brought to pass, and in less than ten years' time an orderly and comprehensive system of common schools was created out of the chaos which had theretofore existed.

---
[1] *Three Years' Residence in Canada*, Vol. II, p. 109.

CHAPTER III.

The District Grammar School—Legislative and Administrative Aspects.

Although in the proceedings, legislative and otherwise, which attended the Royal Land Grant of 1797, definite reference was made to use of this grant for the founding and maintenance of public grammar schools, little was really done in this connection for over forty years. During the meantime, such grammar schools as were established, were, with one exception, supported wholly out of the Provincial treasury. The reasons for this delay and the political dissensions which arose because of it have already been referred to.

A brief review of the Educational Proceedings in the Provincial Legislature prior to 1807 may throw some light upon educational conditions during the period, and will serve incidentally to illustrate the inertia which all important reforms invariably have to overcome.

In 1804, a petition[1] was presented to the Lieutenant-Governor and Legislature from the County of Glengarry, mentioning that the Highlanders who formed practically the total population of the county were extremely backward in promoting education, for two chief reasons: First, that they used the Gaelic language in ordinary intercourse and in their religious services and hence thought an English education unnecessary and, second, that in the mother country they were used to charity schools and were consequently unwilling to go to any personal expense in the matter of educating their children. The petition stated further that, because of these facts, the schools existing in the county were "fluctuating and of little value" and asked on political and moral grounds for the erection of schools on Provincial authority and at Provincial expense.

On the same day that this petition was read in the House of Assembly, a bill was introduced asking for the establishment of district schools out of any funds remaining unappropriated in the Provincial treasury. This bill was lost by the deciding

---
[1] Copy of Petition in *Doc. Hist.*, Vol. I, pp. 47, 48.

vote of the speaker. Later in the session, the member who had been responsible for the measure obtained leave from the House to bring in a bill for the establishment of a school fund. Three days later he was allowed to substitute an address on the subject in place of his projected bill. Almost immediately thereafter he left for his home, so that even the address failed to find its way before the House.

In 1805, the member in question—a Mr. Ebenezer Washburn—re-introduced his bill for establishing district schools. The House, however, proceeded no further in the matter than the holding of two meetings to consider the measure in committee of the whole. A bill for the purchase of "Philosophical Apparatus" met a somewhat similar fate, being dropped at the end of its second reading. It would appear from the records of their deliberations, that the Legislative Council during these two years was even less interested in educational legislation than was the House, nothing of the kind having been attempted by them.

The legislative session of 1806 witnessed a decided step in advance in the matter of education. At an early period in the session, the House in Committee of the Whole passed a resolution to the effect that "Seminaries for the education of the youth are highly necessary in this Province."[1] The bill for the purchase of "Philosophical Apparatus" being re-introduced, passed both branches of the Legislature and was assented to by the Lieutenant-Governor. This bill, as enacted, set apart £400 for the purpose mentioned and provided that "the said instruments" should be deposited "in the hands of some person employed in the education of youth in this Province, in order that they may be as useful as the state of the Province will permit."[2] Some idea of this apparatus and the work which it accomplished is given in the following quotation from a local historian who, writing many years later, said, "From the débris of which collection preserved in one of the rooms of the Home District School building, we ourselves, like others, probably, of our contemporaries, obtained our very earliest inkling of the existence and significance of scientific apparatus."[3]

---

[1] *Doc. Hist.*, Vol. I, p. 52.
[2] 46th George III, Chap. III, "An act to procure certain apparatus, etc.," *Doc. Hist.*, Vol. I, p. 56.
[3] Dr. Scadding in "Toronto of Old," quoted in *Doc. Hist.*, Vol. I, p. 55.

Grammar School—Legislative and Administrative Aspects. 35

As to grammar school legislation, nothing was achieved in this year. A bill entitled "An act for the more general dissemination of learning throughout this Province" while it passed the House, failed to secure the endorsement of the Council. A similar bill, however, became law in the following year, under the title "An act to establish public schools in each and every district of this Province." Because of the importance of this measure it will be necessary to give it a somewhat detailed consideration.

By the Act of 1807[1] the Province was divided for school purposes into eight districts, as against four as recommended by the special committee which dealt with the matter in 1798 and whose report is referred to in a preceding chapter. These eight districts were as follows: The Western District with a school at Sandwich, the London District with a school to be situated in the Township of Townshend, the Niagara District with a school at Niagara, the Home District with a school at York (now Toronto), the Midland District with a school at Kingston, the Johnstown District with a school in the township of Augusta and the Eastern District with a school at Cornwall. The reader who is acquainted with the geography of Ontario will see that these districts extended along the southern border of the Province from the Detroit river on the west almost to the Ottawa river on the east. Thus each district embraced an area which is now occupied by several counties.

The salary of the master of each school was fixed by the Act at £100 yearly payable out of the Provincial treasury upon an order of the Lieutenant-Governor upon the Receiver-General. To the Lieutenant-Governor was assigned also the duty of appointing not less than five trustees for each district and of ratifying or rejecting the teachers which these trustees might select for their respective districts. The trustees as representing, in a sense, the local community, were vested with the right of examining and appointing teachers, subject, as mentioned above, to the approval of the Lieutenant-Governor. They were also given the power of removing at their discretion any teacher " for any misdemeanor or impropriety of conduct," and of nominating a successor. In addition, they were authorized to make

---
[1] 47 George III, Chap. VI, "An act to establish Public Schools in each and every District of this Province." *Doc. Hist.*, Vol. I, p. 70.

"such rules and regulations for the good government and management of the said public schools with respect to the teacher, for the time being, and to the scholars, as in their discretion shall seem meet."

Although it is not expressly stated in the Act, it is to be presumed that the trustees were held responsible for the provision of the necessary school buildings and equipment. In fact these already existed in the case of three of the schools—those at Cornwall, Kingston and York. In one case at least—that of the District of London—there is a record of a popular subscription being taken up for the building of a school house.[1] The schools in question were not free in the present sense of the term as applied to education. Tuition fees were charged which went to swell the salary of the master, who was also, in some cases at least, allowed to further supplement his income by taking scholars as boarders. The Act was to be in force for four years from the date of its passing but in the following year this restriction was removed and it became a permanent piece of legislation.

It would appear that there was little delay in giving effect to the provisions of the Act, since the Lieutenant-Governor, Sir Francis Gore, in his Speech from the Throne at the opening of Parliament in 1808, was able to make the following announcement: "Since the last session of this Legislature, the necessary means have been taken on my part, and on that of the trustees appointed by me, for the establishing of public schools, institutions which I trust, will be the means not only of communicating useful knowledge to the youth of this Province, but also of instilling into their minds principles of religion and loyalty."[2] The House of Assembly expressed itself in its reply as follows: "We highly applaud the prompt and efficacious measures adopted by Your Excellency and we pleasingly anticipate from these institutions the most substantial benefits to the rising generation in this Province."[3]

The satisfied state of mind reflected in these words was not, however, to continue very long. During this very session, three members of the House left their seats and departed for their

---

[1] *Vide* Petition to the House of Assembly from certain inhabitants of the London District in *Doc. Hist.*, Vol. I, p. 71.
[2] *Doc. Hist.*, Vol. I, p. 62.
[3] *Doc. Hist.*, Vol. I, p. 62.

Grammar School—Legislative and Administrative Aspects.

homes in order (ineffectually, as it turned out) to prevent the assembling of a quorum and the consequent passing of the bill which removed the four years' restriction from the act of the preceding year. Local disapproval of a policy which concentrated the government patronage upon a single school in a district was shown by the presentation to both branches of the Legislature, of a numerously signed petition from the London District asking that the legislative grant to that district be divided among four schools instead of being used for the support of a single one.

The spirit which prompted this petition re-asserted itself in two petitions presented at the legislative session of 1812, one from the Newcastle and one from the Midland District. The two were similar in tone but the latter was the more explicit in its statement of grievances.

> By reason of the place of instruction being established at one end of the District and the sum demanded for tuition, in addition to the annual contribution received from the public, most of the people are unable to avail themselves of the advantages contemplated by the institution. A few wealthy inhabitants and those of the town of Kingston reap exclusively the benefit of it in this District. The institution, instead of aiding the middling and poorer classes of His Majesty's subjects, casts money into the lap of the rich, who are sufficiently able, without public assistance, to support a school in every respect equal to the one established by law. Your Petitioners . . . cannot be persuaded that you will continue in force an Act proved by a fair experiment to be so partial in its operation, and so little calculated to effect the contemplated objects.

Thus spoke the voice of Democracy. The aristocratic attitude in regard to public education found expression in a counter-petition from the Eastern District addressed to the Lieutenant-Governor in person: "We have seen provision made for giving the youth of this Province such a liberal education, as may not only qualify them for the learned professions, but also establish firmly in their minds the purest morals and religious principles, which shall enable them to give the most salutary direction to the general manners of the Province, and revive that ardent patriotism, for which their fathers have been so honorably distinguished."[1]

Although by the Common Schools Act of 1816, a rather liberal provision was made for the endowment of elementary education,

---
[1] Copies of the three petitions referred to are given in *Doc. Hist.*, Vol. I, pp. 76, 77.

the attention of the popular branch of the Legislature was not to be diverted thereby from the question of grammar school reform.

During the session of 1817, a bill "to repeal part of and to amend the laws now in force for establishing district schools, etc.," passed the House of Assembly. It was amended by the Legislative Council and returned for the further consideration of the House. The sudden proroguing of Parliament by the Lieutenant-Governor, Sir Francis Gore, prevented any definite action of the House on the amended bill.

In the following year (1818) a grammar school amendment bill was again introduced in the House. It was subsequently dropped to make room for a grammar school repeal bill. This latter bill went no further than a first reading and so the amendment bill was brought forward once more and passed, under the title "An act to repeal part of and amend the laws now in force for establishing district grammar schools in the districts of this Province and further to amend the provisions of the same." This bill was amended by the Council, accepted in its amended form by the House and to become law lacked only the assent of the interim Lieutenant-Governor, the Honorable Samuel Smith. This gentleman, however, possibly because of the temporary character of his office, withheld that assent until he had obtained "the signification of His Majesty's pleasure in Council thereon."[1] This action prevented the enactment of the bill into law since no effort was apparently made to consult the Royal Will in the matter, possibly because of the appointment a few months thereafter of a new Lieutenant-Governor, Sir Peregrine Maitland.

On account of the impoverished state of the Provincial treasury, the new Executive found it necessary to call an extra session of the Legislature. At this session, although matters of finance were naturally uppermost, sufficient attention was paid to education to result in the passing by the House of a Grammar School Amendment bill identical in title with that of the previous session. A conference between committees of the two houses, in regard to possible amendments, was in progress when the Lieutenant-Governor, having secured the necessary grants, dissolved Parliament.

---
[1] Minutes of House for 1st April, 1818, in *Doc. Hist.*, Vol. I, p. 118.

Grammar School—Legislative and Administrative Aspects. 39

The exact nature of these various bills and amendments cannot be determined. Some inkling of their character, may, however, be obtained from a study of the Grammar School Amendment Act of 1819. The Act in question is significant not so much for any important reforms which it inaugurated as for the important tendencies which it illustrates. We will proceed to a brief analysis of this measure.

The germ of local supervision of the instruction of the school is found in a clause which directs that the trustees in each district shall cause "a public examination of their respective schools to be held previous to the annual vacation,[1] at which they or a majority of them shall assist." The strengthening of Parliamentary control of the school system is indicated by the provision that annual reports shall be made from each district to the Lieutenant-Governor and that these reports are to be by him laid before the Legislature "at its first meeting, for their inspection."[2] The enlargement of the scope of the grammar schools is secured by a clause which provides that in every district there shall be educated at the grammar school gratis ten children to be selected by lot from a larger number to be nominated by the trustees of the various common schools in the same district. In order to guard against an insufficient return from the government grant of one hundred pounds to each school it is provided that in future grammar school masters in districts where the average attendance does not exceed ten are to receive only fifty pounds per annum.[3]

During the twenty years between 1819 and 1839, there was very little legislation directly affecting the grammar schools. One new school—that of the Gore District—had been added to the original eight by the Act of 1819. Two more—in the Ottawa District and the Bathurst District—were created in 1823. In addition to these, Upper Canada College, a (so-called) superior grammar school, was founded by the Lieutenant-Governor, Sir John Colborne, in 1829. The interest of the Legislature in private schools is illustrated by a loan of two hundred and fifty pounds made in 1837, to the Grantham Academy at

---
[1] 59th George III, Chap. IV, "An Act to repeal part of, and to amend, the law now in force for establishing Public (Grammar) Schools in the Several Districts of this Province and to extend the provisions of the same." Sec. 4, *Doc. Hist.*, Vol. I, pp. 148-49.
[2] *Ibid.*, Sec. 5.
[3] *Ibid.*, Secs. 6, 7.

St. Catherines to enable it to liquidate a pressing debt. This act is significant as being the earliest step in a policy which the government of the Province has pursued down to the present day—that of granting financial aid to private institutions which for any reason are deemed to merit such assistance.

Certain changes, were, however, made in the administration of the grammar schools. In 1823, on authority from Earl Bathurst, the Colonial Secretary, a General Board of Education was appointed by the Executive with powers of supervision over both the grammar and the common schools.[1] Although the existence and functions of this board were recognized by the Common School Act of 1824 it was made, during the ten years of its existence, the object of more than one attack in the House of Assembly. The reasons for these attacks as well as the determination of the House to assert its right to a share in the administration of the schools are illustrated by the following quotations from a report, made in 1832, of a Select Committee of that body on Education.

We trust that Your Excellency regarding the importance of Economy, will not continue the appropriation of three hundred pounds (£300) a year to a President of a General Board of Education—a Board which can be of no use if the District Boards of Education are constituted of persons active, zealous and conscientious in the discharge of the duties appertaining to their appointment.

By the present law the District (Grammar) School Reports ought to be made directly to Your Excellency by whom they are laid before the Legislature.

No systems are improved by being made more complicated; and the objection acquires greater force from the consequent increase in the number of officers drawing upon the revenue devoted to Education and from the diminished importance of the Local Boards of Education, whose activity and usefulness will vary with the respect following their independence and direct responsibility to your Excellency.[2]

Another and perhaps a stronger reason for the opposition to which we have referred was the fact that the General Board of Education had stood for the supremacy of the Established Church in the field of public education, even going to the extent of using school land for the endowment of Church of England National Schools throughout the Province. This persistent hos-

---
[1] *Vide* copy of letter from Earl Bathurst, Colonial Secretary, authorizing the appointment of a General Board of Education, *Doc. Hist.*, Vol. I, p. 180.
[2] From Report of Select Com. on Ed. as formulated in an address to Lieutenant Governor Sir John Colborne.—*Doc. Hist.*, Vol. I, pp. 272–273.

tility on the part of the House of Assembly had its effect, for in a Confidential Despatch, dated July 1832, Lord Goderich, the Colonial Secretary, directs the Lieutenant-Governor, Sir John Colborne, "to take the necessary legal measures for dissolving the Board and of re-investing in the Crown the estate of which they have had charge."[1] These instructions were carried out and the Board formally dissolved in the following year (1833). No real change, however, was wrought by this act of the Executive. The functions formerly performed by the Board were transferred to the Council of King's College. The membership of the two bodies was almost identical and the Archdeacon of York, the Reverend Doctor Strachan, was president of the Council as he had been of the Board before its dissolution.

This transfer of authority received, so far as the grammar schools were concerned, legislative sanction in the Grammar School Act of 1839. Under this Act, as has been already mentioned, the grammar schools were endowed with two hundred and fifty thousand acres of waste land. The revenue accruing from this land was to be distributed by the Council of King's College in the following manner: One hundred pounds was to be paid annually, as thitherto, to the trustees of the various districts, and, at the discretion of the Council, there might be granted a further amount to be used in providing "an additional master and other means of instruction."[2]

The Act provided further that district trustees might also receive from the General School Fund two hundred pounds to "aid in the erection of a suitable building for a school house in each district: Provided an equal sum shall be raised by subscription among the inhabitants for a like object and provided they shall ensure the permanent insurance of such building."[3]

In the clause just quoted we have the first specific declaration of a principle so characteristic of the later educational policy of the Province—that of the co-operation of the Government with the local community not only in the payment of teachers and the supervision of the schools but also in the erection and equipment of school buildings. The adoption of this principle

---
[1] Copy of Despatch in *Doc. Hist.*, Vol. II, pp. 85-87.
[2] 2nd Victoria, Chap. X. "An Act to Provide for the Advancement of Education in this Province," Sec. 5.—*Doc. Hist.*, Vol. III, p. 170.
[3] *Ibid.*, Sec. 7.

paved the way for the establishment at a later date of certain minimum requirements as to school buildings, grounds and equipment which must be complied with before the Government grant can become available.

Opportunity for grammar school expansion was given by the Act in a clause which states: "It shall and may be lawful for the Lieutenant-Governor to authorize a sum not exceeding One Hundred Pounds (£100) per annum for each school, to be paid to any Board of Trustees, for the use and support of two other schools than the one in the Town where the Court House is situated, in any Town or Village in which the inhabitants shall provide a suitable school house, at which not less than sixty (60) scholars shall be educated: Provided any such additional school shall not be within six miles of the District Town; and provided always, that nothing herein contained shall prevent the Council of King's College from extending aid to four Grammar Schools (including the said two) other than the one established in the District Town should the said Council deem it expedient."[1] An incidental provision which is worthy of notice was the formal adoption of the term "Grammar" as applied to these schools to the exclusion of the names "District" and "Public" which had theretofore been used.

Although the first parliament which met after the union of Upper and Lower Canada in 1841 provided for a reorganization of the common school system, it did little for the grammar schools beyond continuing the conditions which already existed. Certain minor changes, were, however, effected. While the management of the grammar school lands was left with the Council of King's College, the disbursement of the revenue from these lands and the general control of the schools themselves was transferred to the Executive. This latter change was doubtless due to a widespread dissatisfaction in the various districts with the character of the rules and regulations which had been drawn up by the Council for the government of the grammar schools. Such important reforms as the consolidation of the grammar and elementary schools into one system under the expert supervision of a Superintendent of Public Instruction, the enlargement of the powers of the Municipal Councils and of the local

---

[1] 2nd Victoria, Chap. X, "An Act to Provide, etc.," Sec. 8.

trustees, the framing of a course of study more in keeping with modern conditions of life and the fixing of the qualifications of grammar school masters, remained for the Act of 1853 to accomplish. Any detailed discussion of that act[1] would manifestly be outside the province of this present study as would be also any attempt to trace the legislation which, from that date to the present time, has enlarged upon the principles which were there laid down.

---
[1]For such a discussion, *vide* Ross, *School System of Ontario*, pp. 113-115.

CHAPTER IV.

THE DISTRICT GRAMMAR SCHOOL—ITS PECULIAR FEATURES.

We may now proceed to a brief description of the actual working of the district grammar schools since such is necessary to any definite conclusion as to the place which they filled in the social and educational life of the period.

In England, as is well known, much of the fame and not a little of the efficiency of certain of the great public schools has arisen from the inseparable association with them of the names of a few great masters, such as Arnold and Temple of Rugby, Thring of Uppingham, Hawtrey of Eton and Bradley of Marlborough. In the history of the district grammar schools only one name stands pre-eminently forth, that of the Reverend John Strachan, master in turn of the schools at Cornwall and York. A graduate of King's College, Aberdeen, and a schoolmaster of some experience in Scotland he came to Upper Canada, as has already been said, to take charge of the university planned by Governor Simcoe. The recall and departure of that official before Mr. Strachan had reached the Province left the latter upon his arrival without any visible means of support. According to his own story he would have returned to Scotland forthwith if he only had had the money for his passage. To provide himself a livelihood, he became, for the time being, a tutor in the family of the Honorable Richard Cartwright of Kingston. His success in that work paved the way for the opening of a school at Cornwall which subsequently (in 1806) became the grammar school of the Eastern District. Thither in a few years resorted the youth of many of the prominent families of the Province and from this school went out young men who were to occupy leading positions in the church, at the bar, in politics and in commercial life. A contemporary account of a public examination held in this school in 1805 is of interest as giving in some detail the curriculum of the institution.

The students underwent in their different classes a rigid examination, as well at the instance of the gentlemen of learning who attended as of the Reverend Preceptor, in the following order: The Latin Classics,

District Grammar School—Its Peculiar Features. 45

Arithmetic, Book-keeping, Elements of Mathematics, Elements of Geography, of Natural and Civil History. The boys acquitted themselves with great credit; neither is it easy to declare in which branch of learning they succeeded best. The whole was interspersed with different pieces of poetry and prose, many of the most humorous cast, composed for the occasion.[1]

Mr. Strachan, it may be mentioned, had a penchant for versifying and his compositions (invariably in the heroic couplet form, it would appear) occupied during his head-mastership a prominent place in the public exercises of the two schools mentioned. Another feature which came to be characteristic of these exercises was the reproduction in an abbreviated form of famous debates of the British Houses of Parliament. Certain portions of selected speeches were memorized and recited by the older boys, the form of the debate being carefully preserved. This practice was supposed to give to the boys training in public speaking. That it helped to make ready orators of them is open to question, though it must have given them some understanding of parliamentary procedure while it doubtless encouraged in many an ambition to participate in political life.

Mr. Strachan was certainly a teacher of marked ability. One of his pupils, speaking many years later, bears this testimony: " He was an excellent instructor. His scholars were deeply grounded in their work. The grammar was well mastered and every rule thereof deeply impressed on the memory. Every lesson was thoroughly dissected and everything connected with it thoroughly understood before we passed to another lesson."[2]

In many respects Mr. Strachan was far in advance of his time in educational theory. The curriculum which we have just quoted gives evidence of his interest in geography and in " Natural and Civil History." This interest is doubtless due to the fact that in his student days these subjects had a decided attraction for him. So proficient did he become in them, indeed, that he was offered a position as assistant to the Reverend James Brown, Professor of Natural Philosophy in the University of Glasgow. Mr Strachan was to perform the experiments which were to accompany the lectures. The unexpected retirement of the professor prevented the realization of this project and the

---
[1] From the *Upper Canada Gazette and Canadian Oracle* of August 4th, 1805, quoted in *Doc. Hist.*, Vol. I, p. 24.
[2] Bishop Fuller in a Sermon on the death of Bishop Strachan, *Journal of Education for Upper Canada*, Vol. XX (1867), p. 183.

disappointment ensuing had, it would appear, not a little to do with Mr. Strachan's acceptance of the offer of a position in the New World.

Mr. Strachan's rather liberal views as to the curriculum are further illustrated in a course of study which he suggested, in 1829, for the grammar schools of the Province. This course included besides Latin and Greek, which naturally occupied the foremost place: (1) English, under which was placed,—Spelling; Writing; Grammar and Composition; Elocution; Civil and Natural History; Geography, Ancient and Modern; Use of the Globes; Construction of Maps; (2) Mathematics, which comprised Arithmetic; Book-keeping; Algebra; Euclid; Trigonometry; Application to heights and distances; Surveying; Navigation; Dialling; Elements of Astronomy, etc.; (3) French, which was to be studied during four of the five years of the course.[1] After outlining the course, Mr. Strachan (then the Archdeacon of York and a Doctor of Divinity) made the following comment: " In presenting a detailed account of the mode of carrying this course of study into effect, I do not indulge in any imaginary process but give the actual practice of a school which flourished twenty-five years in this province." (Alluding of course to the Home District Grammar School.)

Of Mr. Strachan's methods as a teacher, Dr. Scadding of Toronto, in a biographical sketch, gives the following interesting account.

In (his) system the practical and the useful were by no means sacrificed to the ornamental and theoretical or the merely conventional. Things were regarded as well as words. . . . In regard to things—the science of common objects—we doubt if in the most complete of our modern schools there was ever awakened a greater interest or intelligence in relation to such matters. Who that has once participated in the excitement of its natural history class ever forgot it? Or in that of the historical or geographical exercises? We venture to think that in many an instance the fullest experience of after life, in travel or otherwise, had often their association with ideas awakened then; and often compared satisfactorily and pleasurably with the pictures of persons, animals and places given rudely as it may be in text-books ransacked and conned in a fervor of emulation then. The manner of study in these subjects was this: Each lad was required to prepare a set of questions to be put by himself to his fellows in the class. If a reply was not forthcoming and

---

[1] Letter of Dr. Strachan to the Rev. A. N. Bethune, quoted in *Doc. Hist.*, Vol. I, p. 110.

District Grammar School—Its Peculiar Features. 47

the information furnished by the questioner was judged correct, the latter "went up" and took the place of the other. This process besides being instructive and stimulating to the pupils, possessed the advantage of being, as is often proved, highly diverting to the teacher.[1]

It must not be supposed, however, that Mr. Strachan was wholly free from the defects which were characteristic of the schools of his time both in the Old World and in the New. The paragraph just quoted illustrates the fact that he sought to develop among his pupils a spirit of emulation and competition rather than one of helpful co-operation. Moreover he employed at times other incentives to progress and studious behavior which are still more at variance with the best thought of the present day. "Now and then," says Dr. Scadding, in a book of reminiscences, "a boy would be seen standing at one of the posts with his jacket inside out; or he might be seen there in a kneeling posture for a number of minutes, or standing with the arm extended holding a book."[2]

The two masters who in turn governed the Home District Grammar School between the date of Mr. Strachan's resignation of the office and 1829, the date of the absorption of the school by Upper Canada College, are both of them worthy of at least a passing notice. The first was Mr. Samuel Armour, a graduate of the University of Glasgow, "very much of a sportsman" so that when, during school hours, flocks of wild pigeons passed over the town and the sound of the firing of guns could be heard on all sides, "his attention would be very much drawn off from the class subjects." It was this Mr. Armour who, when there was only one copy of Eutropius available for use in the school, safeguarded the scholarship and the morals of his pupils by stitching together the leaves of the English translation, which was bound along with the Latin text.

Following Mr. Armour was the Reverend Thomas Phillips, a graduate of Queen's College, Cambridge, "the very ideal outwardly of an English country parson of the old type," and who "wore powder in the hair except when in mourning." It was he who introduced into the school the Eton Latin Grammar which superseded "Rudiman's Rudiments," a book "which really did give hints of something rational underlying what we learned

[1] *The First Bishop of Toronto—a Review and a Study.*
[2] *Toronto of Old*, p. 11.

out of it." The Eton Greek Grammar "in its purely mediaeval and untranslated state also made its appearance. Our 'Palaephatus' and other extracts in the Graeca Minora were translated by us not into English but into Latin, in which language all the notes and elucidations of difficulties in that book were given. Very many of the Greek 'genitives absolute,' we remember, were to be rendered by 'quum' with the subjunctive pluperfect, an enormous mystery to us at the time." It is small wonder that Dr. Scadding, from whom we have been quoting,[1] adds the sententious remark "The *Chevaux de frise* set up across our pathway to knowledge were numerous and most forbidding." Upon the establishment of Upper Canada College the Reverend Mr. Phillips was made the Vice-Principal of that institution.

A brief reference to conditions in some of the other grammar schools of the province may be in place here. A citizen of the town of Kingston, writing in 1814 to the editor of the *Kingston Gazette* makes the following comment on the local grammar school:

It must be peculiarly gratifying to the public in general to see how completely the plan of the government has been carried into effect in the institution of the public schools throughout this province.[2]

The success which this school in particular has met with has exceeded the most sanguine expectations. Youths not yet sixteen have gone as far as equations in Algebra—by no means imperfectly—and are well versed in the principles of Geometry and in the theory and practice of plane trigonometry. Their progress in Greek and Latin is no less surprising.

That the grammar school of the Eastern District (situated at Cornwall) maintained, in a measure at least, the high standard set for it by its first master, Dr. Strachan, is shown by the fact that, in 1827, its master, the Reverend Hugh Urquhart was able to report as follows: "Four boys read in Ovid's Metamorphoses and are ready to begin Sallust. Seven read in Adams' Select Lessons and are ready to commence the Lives of Cornelius Nepos. Six are finishing Rudiman's Rudiments, one boy is reading Virgil."

"Of the remaining twelve boys, five are learning English grammar and reading Murray's Introduction; five are spelling

---
[1] *Toronto of Old*, pp. 166–169.
[2] Letter to the Editor of the *Kingston Gazette* dated 20th June, 1814. Quoted in *Doc. Hist.*, Vol. I, p. 83.

words of four or five letters in Mavor's Spelling Book; two confine their attention exclusively to Writing and Arithmetic. All the Latin boys are exercised twice a week in Geography (Ancient and Modern) and four times a week in Arithmetic."[1]

A disposition on the part of many parents to send their children to the United States to complete their education is noticed by several writers of the period, some of whom are careful to point out the dangers, both civic and moral, which such a course might involve. This tendency is illustrated in the case of the Ottawa District Grammar School. In 1827 the master of that school reports as follows: " Since I had the honour of reporting before on the state of the school, the scholars studying Greek and Latin under me have left the school and no others have yet supplied their place; they have gone to Burlington College in the United States there being a great tendency in this place to send their children to finish their education in the States."[2]

Apparently the least successful of all the grammar schools was that of the Western District situated at the town of Sandwich. In 1828, the trustees reported to the House of Assembly that, partly because of the unhealthfulness of the town which prevented scholars being sent there from a distance, and partly because of the illiteracy of the neighboring farmers and their consequent inability " to appreciate a liberal education," the school " is composed principally of very young children learning the first rudiments of the English language, and among the five classical scholars there is but one at all advanced; the rest have only commenced within six or eight months."[3]

An advertising card of the Johnstown District Grammar School (situated at Brockville), issued in March, 1839, is of interest because of the information which it gives about fees, boarding regulations and holidays. The card is quoted in full.

This Institution is now under the care of the Reverend Henry Caswell, A. M., assisted by a competent Instructor.

1. For Board and Tuition in the usual branches £30 per annum. Each boarder will provide for his washing, and is expected to be supplied with a Bed and Bedding, Towels and a Silver Spoon. Theological pupils boarding with the Principal will pay £50 per annum, and will receive, separately from the other pupils, such instructions in Divinity as the

---

[1] Reports from District Grammar Schools, 1827, given in *Doc. Hist.*, Vol. I, pp. 227 and seq.
[2] *Ibid.*
[3] *Doc. Hist.*, Vol. I, p. 301.

Ecclesiastical Authority may appoint with the addition of Hebrew and Chaldee, if desired.

2. For instructions in Spelling, Reading and English Grammar, Arithmetic, Geography, History and Writing £4 per annum.

3. For instruction in Greek, Latin, Mathematics, Natural Philosophy, Composition, etc., £5 per annum. All accounts must be settled at Midsummer and Christmas. The full quarter is charged if the pupil is once entered. No deduction is allowed except at the discretion of the Principal.

The hours of attendance are from 9 to 3 o'clock with an intermission of half an hour. The vacations are: four weeks at Midsummer, three at Christmas and one at Easter.[1]

The remaining grammar schools of the Province were, it would seem, very similar in their general features to the one which has just been described, hence without further elaboration or quotation we may proceed to a summary of the chief characteristics which the grammar school as an institution exhibited. This summary will, of course, be little more than a re-statement of facts already presented.

(1) It was, in the main, a boarding school, though the school at York, on account of that place being the seat of Government, was also largely patronized by day-pupils; hence, in addition to the grant from the Government and the tuition fees which he received, the income of the master was generally considerably augmented by charges made for the boarding of pupils.

(2) They were mainly in charge of clergymen who were most frequently of the Anglican and Presbyterian communions. The bearings of this fact are discussed in some detail in another connection.

(3) They were mainly for the children of the well-to-do. The provision of the Act of 1819 that ten poor children should be educated gratis at each district grammar school did little if anything to change the aristocratic character of these schools. In fact, Dr. Strachan, in 1832, made the following statement before a Select Committee of the House of Assembly on Education: "No district has, I believe, availed itself of this privilege nor will they until the School Fund or the Legislature assume the whole expense of such scholars while they remain

---

[1] *Doc. Hist.*, Vol. IV., p. 156.

District Grammar School—Its Peculiar Features. 51

at the District Grammar Schools in board and lodging as well as in tuition."[1]

(4) They adhered as closely as their circumstances would permit to the classical traditions of their prototypes in the mother country. In fact, it was not till 1853 that Latin and Greek were dethroned from their place at the head of the curriculum and it was not till 1871 that the name "grammar school" gave way to the more modern name of "high school."

Reference has already been made in this chapter to Upper Canada College "the superior grammar school" founded in 1829 by Sir John Colborne. It has been mentioned in the discussion of the Land Grant for Schools, since, at its establishment, it was assigned 66,000 acres of land from the university endowment. Its relation to the Anglican Church and the difficulties which arose therefrom will be dealt with in a subsequent chapter. It will be sufficient here to show wherein it differed from the district grammar schools.

In the first place it was a much closer approximation to the public schools of England, being directly patterned after Elizabeth College in the Island of Guernsey, an institution which had been founded, or rather re-founded in 1826 by Sir John Colborne himself. Upper Canada College was, in the second place, a much more pretentious institution than even the largest of the grammar schools (that of the Home District) had been. In fact its establishment led to the discontinuance for some seven years of the Home District School. The principal and his four leading associates were all graduates of Oxford or Cambridge, and three of these five men had achieved high honors at their respective universities. Of these men and the influence which they exerted, Dr. Scadding in a memorial volume published in 1884 and styled *Toronto, Past and Present*, says: "They were all of them instrumental in inaugurating and fostering in Upper Canada a species of scholarship which is peculiarly English. The jar long retains the odour of the wine with which when new it was first filled. To this day there lingers here and there in Canada, Upper and Lower, some of the aroma of

---

[1] From evidence given by Dr. Strachan before the Select Committee of the House of Assembly on Education 1832. In *Doc. Hist.*, Vol. II, p. 88.

the old Massie first supplied to the country by Dr. Harris and his colleagues."[1]

Upper Canada College during the thirteen years of its history with which we are immediately concerned certainly performed a valuable work, since throughout that period it was the only College within the Province. In fact, as has already been mentioned, the House of Assembly was at one time anxious, because of the many restrictions contained in the King's College Charter of 1827, to create out of Upper Canada College a Provincial university with a charter far more liberal than the one to which so much exception had been taken.

The limitations of Upper Canada College were, however, of a serious nature and led to opposition from at least three different quarters.

I. There was an element in the local community which objected to the purely classical character of the curriculum. The sentiment of these people was voiced in a petition to the Lieutenant-Governor asking for such changes in the character of the instruction "as will enable Your Excellency's petitioners and others in similar circumstances to have their sons educated in a college in such branches of an English education as will qualify them for discharging, with efficiency and respectability, the scientific and other business of tradesmen and mechanics."[2] In consequence of this petition and of an active propaganda of the views contained in it, provision was finally made, to use the words of Principal Harris, for the introduction of "a greater proportion of miscellaneous (not classical, that is,) studies especially in the lower part of the College."

II. There was strong opposition to the College from the inhabitants of other districts of Upper Canada. They felt, and rightly, that too great a proportion of the educational revenues of the Province were being expended for the benefit of the town of York and especially for the benefit of a certain aristocratic element in that town. This opposition found frequent expression both in the House of Assembly and elsewhere. The most outspoken critic of all was Mr. William Lyon Mackenzie, a member of the House of Assembly during several sessions, at one time Mayor of York and for many years editor of *The Colonial*

---
[1] *Op. cit.*, p. 109.
[2] Copy of petition given in *Doc. Hist.*, Vol. II, p. 29.

Advocate, a radical newspaper. Mackenzie was a man of great intellectual ability and of entire honesty of purpose but, unfortunately for himself and others, he was decidedly lacking in judgment. In his anxiety to overthrow "The Family Compact" as the small circle of officeholders and influential advisers of the Lieutenant-Governor was called, he planned and in fact began an armed *coup d'etat*. The "Mackenzie Rebellion" failed almost before it had begun and he himself and his lieutenants were forced to flee to the United States. The "Rebellion" served at least this useful purpose: it called the attention of the Imperial Parliament to certain flagrant evils in the government of Upper Canada and had not a little to do with causing the investigations undertaken by Imperial Command, by Lord Durham, which investigations, as is well known, prepared the way for the advent of responsible government in both the Canadas.

The following extracts from "Articles of Impeachment or Public Accusations . . . Against the Lieutenant-Governor of the Province and the Advisers of the Crown," published in *The Colonial Advocate* in January, 1832, will show the grounds of Mr. Mackenzie's criticisms of the Lieutenant-Governor's educational policy and will also serve incidentally as an example of his vigorous style.

He (i. e. Sir John Colborne) has endeavored to lay the foundation of a dangerous system of education.

(1) By desiring the Vice-Chancellor of the University of Oxford to elect "the Principal and most of the Masters" of the Provincial College (i. e. of Upper Canada College), although that Vice-Chancellor and the institution over which he presides are bitterly opposed to the patriotic and liberal Cabinet of His Majesty, and although Oxford has been justly characterized as a sanctuary where exploded systems and obsolete prejudices find shelter and protection.

(2) By conducting the affairs of the College in this Town on a narrow, bigoted and sectarian plan, calculated to rise up a class of educated men opposed to the liberal principles of the British Government and wedded to the aristocratic notions of the fallen Tory oligarchy.

(3) By arbitrarily blending the Home District School and (Royal) Grammar School with the above dangerous sectarian institution.[1]

III. While Mackenzie's hostility to Upper Canada College was due to considerations of a political nature, there were others

---
[1] Given in *Doc. Hist.*, Vol. II, p. 58.

who withheld their sympathy because they regarded it as a menace to religious liberty and equality. Chief among these were the leaders in the Methodist and Presbyterian denominations. The measures taken by these men to safeguard what they believed to be the rights of their respective churches will be treated in detail in one of the following chapters, hence nothing further need be said on the subject in this place.

CHAPTER V.

THE COMMON SCHOOL—ITS EXTERNAL HISTORY.

We have seen that in the Land Grant of 1797 no provision was made for the endowment of elementary education. The reason for this lay doubtless in the fact that the work of elementary instruction was thought by the political leaders of the time to belong to the family, to the church and to philanthropic exercise rather than to the state. This view continued to exert a powerful influence throughout the entire period now under review.

Formal elementary instruction apparently began in Upper Canada with what were known as Garrison schools. The chaplains of military posts, such as Kingston and Newark, were in the habit of gathering a few children about them whom they instructed in religion and in the rudiments of an English education. Later, when settlements had grown up at various points along the frontier, other private schools were established. These flourished for longer or shorter terms and sought to minister to what their proprietors conceived to be the educational wants of their respective communities. Two or three of these schools attempted instruction in the classics and higher mathematics and hence may be regarded as the embryos from which grammar schools later developed. One such school—that of the Reverend John Strachan at Cornwall—has been mentioned in the chapter immediately preceding. Dr. Hodgins in his *Documentary History of Education in Upper Canada* has collected from the local newspapers of the time a number of the advertisements of these schools. In addition to this he has given a very carefully prepared and rather extensive list of the schools of this class which were in operation in various parts of the Province between 1786 and 1810.[1] Besides the school at Cornwall, to which reference has just been made, two others on this list are referred to as classical schools, one of these having been opened at Kingston in 1786 by the Reverend Dr. Stuart and the other having been established at York in 1802 by Mr. W. W. Baldwin.

---

[1] Vide *Doc. Hist.*, Vol. I, pp. 30, 31.

The remaining schools—some twenty or more—were all plainly elementary in character. Of these one was an evening school opened at Newark (Niagara) in 1797 by a Mr. Richard Cockrel, another was an orphan school founded, in 1799, at St. Catherines, and two others were regular boarding schools. One of these last was kept by a Mr. and Mrs. Tyler, on the Niagara river near Newark. The "card" of this school is sufficiently interesting to deserve a reproduction here.

Mr. and Mrs. Tyler take the liberty of informing the public that on Monday, the 1st of February (1802) they will open their school for young people—Men and Ladies.

They will keep a regular day school and night school. Children of each sex above the age of four years will be received, and the price will be in proportion to the kind of instruction the parents may wish their children to receive.

They will teach in Reading, Writing and Arithmetic; the young ladies will be instructed in all that is necessary for persons of their sex to appear decently and to be useful in the world, and of all that concerns housekeeping, either for those who wish to live in town or country.

The situation is healthy and agreeable, and the house suitable for a number of boarders. People who, during the heat of summer, may be advised to move for change of air will meet with proper lodgings, healthy and cheap boarding.

Finally, nothing shall be neglected for health, instruction, religion and good morals, and they hope their endeavors to satisfy the public will more and more merit protection and encouragement.

Mrs. Tyler having been bred in the line of mantua-maker, will receive and do her endeavors to execute her work in the neatest manner to the satisfaction of those who honor her with their custom.

She embraces this opportunity to render her sincere thanks for the protection she has received this day.[1]

Dr. Ryerson in his *History of the United Empire Loyalists* mentions the fact that elementary schools were early established in all the loyalist communities where the number of settlers was sufficient to make such an undertaking possible. Just what the character of these schools was it is impossible now to determine but they must, from the very nature of the case, have been exceedingly elementary as well as rather intermittent.

As early as 1799, an attempt was made in the Province to secure the exclusion from the schools of uncertificated teachers. In the *Upper Canada Gazette* (the official organ of the Government) for July of that year there appears the following notice:

---

[1] *Doc. Hist.*, Vol. I, p. 33.

"We are happy in being informed that no person will be countenanced or permitted by the Government to teach school in any part of this Province unless he shall have passed an examination before one of our commissioners and receive a certificate from under his hand specifying that he is adequate to the important task of a tutor."[1]

The first instance of a popular attempt to interest the Provincial Legislature in the support of elementary schools appears in 1804 in the petition from certain inhabitants of the County of Glengarry which is referred to in the chapter on "The Land Grant for Schools." This petition, as we have seen, was unavailing as were also the numerous attempts of a similar character throughout the decade which followed. We have noticed in the preceding chapter the agitation for elementary schools which followed close after the passing of the District (Grammar) School Act of 1807 and the sympathy which on the whole the House of Assembly exhibited towards the movement; consequently we may proceed at once to a discussion of the first piece of definite common school legislation—the so-called Common School Act of 1816. This legislation, as has already been remarked, was in the nature of a compromise and was consented to by the Legislative Council on condition that the grammar schools were to remain undisturbed.

The need of the Province as regards elementary education was recognized by the Lieutenant-Governor, Sir Francis Gore, in his Speech from the Throne at the opening of the legislative session for 1816. "The dissemination of letters is," he observed, "of the first importance to every class; and to aid in so desirable an object, I wish to call your attention to some provision for the establishment of schools in each township, which shall afford the first principles to the children of the inhabitants and prepare such of them as may require further instruction, to receive it in the District Schools."[2]

The Common School Act which was foreshadowed in this speech granted £6,000 annually for school purposes to the ten districts into which the Province was at that time divided. The amount apportioned to the several districts varied from two hundred to one thousand pounds. As soon as a competent

[1] *Doc. Hist.*, Vol. I, p. 33.
[2] *Doc. Hist.*, Vol. I, p. 96.

number of persons inhabiting "any Town, Township, Village or Place" should unite and build a school house and engage to furnish twenty scholars or more, they might, after giving due notice, meet and appoint three trustees who should have the authority to examine and appoint a teacher. Such teacher was required to be a natural born subject of Great Britain or to have taken the oath of allegiance and he might be removed by the trustees for any impropriety of conduct and a successor appointed. The trustees were empowered to make rules and regulations for the governing of the school subject to the approval of the District Board of Education to whom also they were to make a report every three months stating the text-books used and the rules in force in the school. Every year, a special report was to be made informing the District Board of the number of scholars, the branches of study taught and the general condition of the school. The District Board was in turn required to compile an annual report to the Lieutenant-Governor to be by him transmitted to the Legislature. These district trustees were to be not less than three nor more than five in number and were to be appointed by the Lieutenant-Governor.

Teachers were to receive their portions of the Provincial grant every six months upon presenting to the District Treasurer a certificate, signed by the local trustees, that they had given acceptable service during that period and that the number of scholars attending their respective schools had not been less than twenty. The grants made to each district under the Act were to be apportioned among the various schools according to the number of scholars in attendance but no district was to receive more than twenty-five pounds annually.

A free text-book system in any district was made possible by the following clause, "That it shall and may be lawful for the District Boards to be appointed in each and every District in this Province to apply such part of the money hereby granted to the several Districts not exceeding one hundred pounds as they shall see fit, for the purchase of proper books for the use of the said common schools, and after having purchased such books to cause them to be distributed for the use of such schools in such manner as to them shall seem meet."[1]

---

[1] 56th George III, Chap. XXXVI, An act granting to His Majesty a sum of money to be applied to the use of Common Schools, etc., Sec. 12.

Common School—Its External History. 59

The Act of 1816 was limited in its operation to four years from the date of its passing. In the discussion, in the Legislature and elsewhere, which accompanied the movement for its re-enactment certain grave defects in its operation were pointed out. A writer in *The Christian Recorder* for April, 1819, alludes to one of these as follows: " The Bill was very much hurt by the insertion of a clause that there should be a school in every town, village or place where twenty scholars could be collected. These loose words admit of a latitude of interpretation which could not have been intended, and multiply schools to an extent which it would require three times the Provincial revenue to support."[1] It is somewhat difficult to reconcile the statement just quoted, with the fact that an investigation in 1820 showed that in certain districts considerable sums of the money available for common school purposes had remained unappropriated.

Whatever may have been the determining cause or causes, the Common School Act of 1820 reduced the annual Provincial grant from six thousand pounds to two thousand five hundred pounds. This reduction was manifestly favored by the Executive since, in his speech from the Throne in opening the Parliament of 1820, the Lieutenant-Governor, Sir Peregrine Maitland, says: " It is neither prudent nor desirable to proceed (with the bill as it is, that is), but measures may possibly be adopted to provide the same good at a more moderate expense."[2] That the good produced was as " moderate " as the expense incurred is scarcely to be doubted by any one who studies with any care the character of the common schools of the time.

The Act of 1820 modified that of 1816 in other respects as follows: (1) The grant to each district was to be equally divided among the teachers of that district with the proviso that no teacher was to receive from the grant more than twelve pounds ten shillings per annum. (2) No warrant was to issue to any District Treasurer till the sums already paid to him had been accounted for. (3) Provision was made for the return to the Receiver-General of any sums remaining unexpended in the hands of the District Treasurers.

The Act, like its predecessor, was limited in its operation to four years. In 1824, the clause of the Act of 1820 restricting

---

[1] Given in *Doc. Hist.*, Vol. I, p. 156.
[2] *Ibid*, p. 169.

the period of its operation to four years, was repealed, the provisions of the Acts of 1816 and 1820 were enlarged to include schools among the Indians of the Province, and one hundred and fifty pounds was appropriated " for the encouragement of Sunday Schools and for affording the means of moral and religious instruction to the more indigent and remote settlements in the several districts throughout the Province."[1]

In one of the sections of this Act there appears also the first indication (in the case of the common schools at least) of a tendency to require of the teacher a certificate of qualification from an authority more central and presumably better qualified to act as an examining body, than the local school trustees. The clause in question reads as follows:

> Every teacher of a Common School before he shall be entitled to receive any portion of public money shall be examined by the Board of Education in the District in which he shall have taught or is about to teach a Common School, or shall obtain a certificate from at least one member of such Board certifying his ability and fitness to teach the same, due regard at all times being had to the degree of education wanting, or to the branches necessary to be taught in the township, village or place in which such teacher hath undertaken, or is about to undertake, to teach a Common School.[2]

The Act of 1824 contained, among other things, the first legislative recognition of a General Board which was to have supervision of public education in the Province and especially of school funds and school lands. The one hundred and fifty pounds granted to Sunday Schools was to be " at the disposal of the general body that is or may be appointed by the Governor, Lieutenant-Governor, or person administering the Government of this Province, for the superintendence of education within the same, to be by them laid out and expended for the purchase of books and tracts designed to afford moral and religious instruction, which said books and tracts, when so purchased, shall be distributed by the said General Board in equal proportion among the several District Boards of Education throughout this Province."[3]

---

[1] 4th George IV, Chap. VIII, An act to make permanent and extend the provisions of the laws now in force for the establishment and regulation of Common Schools throughout this Province, etc., Sec. I.
[2] Section VI of Act.
[3] Sec. II of Act.

At the risk of needless repetition we will proceed to re-state with some amplifications the main facts concerning this important body.

The initiative in the matter of a General Board of Education had, it would appear, come from the Lieutenant-Governor, Sir Peregrine Maitland. From a communication sent by him to his Executive Council in May, 1823, we learn that the formation of such a board had already been suggested to the Colonial Secretary, Earl Bathurst, and that the latter official had "signified his sanction" of the plan proposed. In view of this endorsement of his policy, Sir Peregrine proposed to the Executive Council " the appropriation of some of the lands set apart for the Endowment of the University, in such manner as shall readily and securely create a fund to enable the General Board of Education to enter on its duties either by conveying a portion of lands in trust to the Board of Education (subject in all of its proceedings to the sanction of the Executive Government)—or by such other mode as may to the Committee of Council appear most expedient."[1]

The body in question was appointed by the Lieutenant-Governor this same year, with Dr. Strachan as President. To enable the Board to carry on its work, some one hundred and ninety thousand acres of land—a most liberal allowance it would seem—was assigned to it by " His Majesty's Government." The Board likewise at its first meeting (June 14th, 1823) " directed the President to submit to His Excellency, the Lieutenant-Governor, the propriety of transferring the School Fund, now in the hands of the Receiver-General, to the Treasurer (of the Board) as contingent expenses for stationery, advertisements, etc., which must be immediately incurred."[2]

The agitation by the House of Assembly against the General Board of Education has been described in the last chapter. Mention has also been made of the discontinuance of the Board in 1833 at the instance of the Home Government. The connection of the Board with the so-called " National " schools will be dealt with at some length in a chapter which is to follow. Apart from its efforts on behalf of the schools just named,

---

[1] From letter, dated May 30th, 1823, to Executive Council, given in *Doc. Hist.*, Vol. I, p. 180.
[2] From minutes of first meeting of Board, *Doc. Hist.*, Vol. III, p. 1.

the Board devoted itself mainly to the making of rules for the government of schools, to the prescribing and in some cases to the publishing of text-books for use in the common schools, and to the seconding of the efforts of Sir John Colborne in the establishment of Upper Canada College.

The noteworthy fact about the General Board of Education, and the fact which in the end led to its discontinuance, was the entire absence of any responsibility on its part to the popular branch of the legislature. It could and it did undertake to divert the proceeds of the school lands to purposes of which the House of Assembly cordially disapproved. It could and it did undertake to supersede the common schools established by Parliamentary enactments with a system of schools wholly sectarian in character. Apparently Dr. Egerton Ryerson, subsequently the founder of the present common school system of Ontario, had these circumstances in mind when, in 1833, he offered the following criticism of a proposed piece of legislation.

> The next leading feature of the Bill is the appointment of a General Board of Education. . . . This is proposed to be left to the Governor, Lieutenant-Governor, or person administering the Government; a proposition in our opinion radically objectionable. It makes the system of Education, in theory, a mere engine of the Executive,—a system which is liable to all the abuse, suspicion, jealousy and opposition caused by despotism; and it withholds from the system of Common School education, in its first and prominent feature, that character of common interest and harmonious co-operation, which, as we humbly conceive, are essential to its success, and even to its acceptance with the Province. Education is an object in which the Government as an individual portion of the Province, and the people at large, possess, in some respects, a common interest; consequently they should exercise a joint, or common, control.[1]

The Common School Act of 1824 continued in force until the union of the two provinces of Upper and Lower Canada in 1841. The amount of the annual grant for common schools varied slightly, from time to time, up till 1835, when, by legislative enactment, it was increased to five thousand six hundred and fifty pounds.

We have noticed in a preceding chapter the various attempts made from 1831 onward to secure a land endowment for the common schools; we will now proceed to a brief characteriza-

---

[1] Article in Christian Guardian of 15th of January, 1834, given in *Doc. Hist.*, Vol. II, p. 149.

tion of certain attempts made, during that period to secure a reorganization of the common school system itself. Although for various reasons, which are too complex to be analyzed here, they failed of becoming law, they are significant as showing an educational awakening similar in nature, if not in extent, to that which was taking place about the same time in many parts of the United States.

In 1831, a bill was introduced in the House of Assembly by a Mr. William Buell, Jr., which provided for (1) three superintendents of schools in each township; (2) a District Board of Education consisting of five members chosen by a board of electors made up of representatives from the township superintendents; (3) a division of the Provincial Grant among the various townships according to their population.[1]

At the session of 1833-34 a Mr. Mahlon Burwell brought forward in the Assembly a bill of which the following were the principal features: (1) A General Board of Education and District Boards of Education appointed by the Lieutenant-Governor; (2) a Board of Township School Commissioners to have supervision of the work of the local school trustees; (3) the establishment of a School Fund "to consist of such sum or sums of money as may annually be appropriated by the Legislature out of the Provincial Revenues and the moneys arising from the sale or leasing of common school lands," also of an amount equal to the Legislative appropriations "to be raised by assessment, by order of the Quarter Sessions in their respective districts on the rateable property."[2] Dr. Ryerson in an editorial comment upon this bill[3] remarks that the idea of a local tax corresponding in amount to the Provincial grant is probably borrowed by the author of the bill from New York State. This comment, coming from such a quarter, is significant as foreshadowing the considerable influence which the example of the United States and especially that of the state just named, was to exert upon school legislation in Canada during the next twenty years.

A common school bill passed by the House of Assembly in 1835[4] provided for: (1) Three superintendents of schools in

[1] Copy of Bill *Doc. Hist.*, Vol. II, pp. 34-36.
[2] *Doc. Hist.*, Vol. II, p. 149.
[3] In Article already cited.
[4] See copy of Bill, *Doc. Hist.*, Vol. II, pp. 206-208.

each township with duties as follows: (a) To select three students from the common schools of the township who were to be considered as applicants for admission to the district grammar schools; (b) "to nominate a fit and proper person to be a member of the District Board of Education." (2) A District Board of Education who should (a) provide for the free boarding and tuition at the District Grammar School of a number of scholars not exceeding eight from each county; (b) arrange for a yearly public examination of all the school teachers in each county. (3) An increase of the yearly common school grant to twelve thousand pounds.

The teachers' examinations provided by this bill were to be presided over in each case by the district grammar school master assisted by such members of the District Board as might reside in the county. Certain additions to their regular salaries (one pound, fifteen shillings, and ten shillings respectively) were to be granted to the three teachers who stood highest at this examination. The bill in question was rejected by the Legislative Council and this rejection, along with that of several other important bills which had been passed by the House at this and preceding sessions, led to a prolonged controversy between the two houses and to the publication by the Council of an elaborate defence of its actions.

The House of Assembly had, in connection with the educational deliberations of 1835, felt the need of information as to the school systems of other countries, consequently, in April of that year, three of its members, Dr. Charles Duncombe, Dr. T. D. Morrison and Mr. William Bruce were appointed a committee "to enquire into the system and management of schools and colleges in order to report fully upon the systems of education pursued in the United States."[1]

Dr. Duncombe as the accredited representative of the committee visited, to use his own words, "the Western, Eastern, Middle and some of the Southern states" and made upon his return a rather extensive report.[2] He studied with some care the school systems of Boston, New York, Albany, Philadelphia, Baltimore and Cincinnati. His catalogue of the different kinds

---

[1] Letter, dated 24th of February, 1836, from Commissioners T. D. Morrison and William Bruce to the Speaker of the House of Assembly in *Doc. Hist.*, Vol. II, p. 288.
[2] Report given in full in *Doc. Hist.*, Vol. II, pp. 289–308.

of schools which came under his notice includes: "Infant Schools, City Free Schools, Grammar Schools, Literary Institutes, Eclectic Institutes, High Schools, Monitorial Schools, Lancaster Schools, Manual Labor Schools, Primary Schools and Writing Schools." In addition to the specific duties imposed on him by his instructions, Dr. Duncombe amassed by inquiry and by reading, considerable information as to the educational policies of different European countries, notably Scotland, France and Prussia.

Though he saw much to approve in certain quarters of the United States and noticed a general "spirit of improvement" abroad, yet he was able to testify: "In the United States, so far as I have witnessed and am capable of judging, their common school systems are as defective as our own. They have, according to their public documents, about eighty thousand common school teachers but very few of whom have made any preparation for their duties; the most of them accidentally assume their office as a temporary employment."

In 1836, Dr. Duncombe presented to the House of Assembly, along with the report of which we have just spoken, the draft of a Common School Bill.[1] The leading provisions of this measure were as follows: (1) There should be a General Superintendent of Education for the Province; (2) there should be in each township three school commissioners and three school inspectors. The school commissioners were assigned the duty of dividing the townships into school sections and of co-operating with the inspectors in the examination of teachers. The inspectors, as their name implies, were the official school visitors. (3) The bill anticipated the normal schools of a much later period by providing that, when the yearly school revenue should exceed ten thousand pounds by one thousand pounds or more, such excess should be employed in establishing four schools for the training of teachers—two for men and two for women; (4) school gardens were provided for in a clause which authorized school trustees to purchase or lease "a lot or parcel of land, farming utensils, seeds, grains and grasses for the use, benefit and behoof of that District, for the use of the teachers of the school or to be annually apportioned among the scholars of the

---
[1] *Doc. Hist.*, Vol. II, pp. 309–322.

school; or otherwise employed and occupied for the profit and instruction of the school or parts thereof, in horticulture, agriculture or otherwise, growing plants, fruits, grasses and grains as the trustees, together with the school teacher for the time being, may think fit."[1] (5) School workshops might in a similar way be acquired and employed " for the purpose of enabling the scholars of the school taught in that District profitably to employ a portion of their time in the acquiring a knowledge of (some) mechanical skill, art, business or profession."[2]

It remains now to mention briefly the chief provisions of the Common School Act of 1841.[3] This Act was passed by the first parliament of the united provinces, and in fact, only a few months after the Act of Union had come into effect. This measure can be safely said to have inaugurated a new order of things in regard to the common schools, although many needed reforms were left for future legislation to accomplish.

The more important features of the act in question were: (1) The establishment of a permanent school fund; (2) a grant of fifty thousand pounds annually to common schools; (3) the appointment at a liberal salary of a Superintendent of Education, one of whose duties was " to visit annually each of the Municipal Districts in the Province (now including both Upper and Lower Canada) and ascertain the state of the common schools therein " and who was instructed to labor for " the establishment of uniformity in the conduct of the common schools throughout the Province; (4) the making of special regulations for the organization of schools, the examination of teachers and the distribution of school moneys in incorporated towns and cities; (5) the formulation of certain conditions under which separate schools for Roman Catholics might be established and supported by the school rates paid by Roman Catholic tax-payers.

The first four of these were certainly much-needed reforms. The last was essentially a measure of expediency, made necessary by the fact that the vast majority of the inhabitants of Lower Canada were Roman Catholics. They could not be expected to send their children to Protestant schools and neither Protestants nor Roman Catholics were in favor of the exclusion of

---

[1] *Doc. Hist.* Vol. II, p. 322.
[2] *Ibid.*
[3] 4th and 5th Victoria, Chap. XVIII, An act to repeal certain acts . . and to make provision for the establishment and maintenance of common schools.

religious instruction from the schools, which was the only remaining alternative.

There was important school legislation in 1843 and again in 1846, but this was mainly for the purpose of correcting certain mistakes and making good certain deficiencies in the Act of 1841. Both these measures are summarized in Dr. Ross's well-known work on *The School System of Ontario,* and to that book the reader, anxious to acquaint himself with their specific content, is referred. It would be interesting to follow in detail the important constructive labors of the Reverend Dr. Ryerson, Superintendent of the Schools of Upper Canada from 1844 till 1876, but such an undertaking lies plainly outside of the province of the present study.

CHAPTER VI.

THE COMMON SCHOOL—ITS ESSENTIAL CHARACTERISTICS.

When we turn to a consideration of the character of common school education between 1816 and 1841, we find a considerable mass of material bearing on the subject, but little that lends itself to systematic classification and arrangement. Hence such conclusions as may be drawn here, will necessarily be quite general in character.

We may say at the outset that the schoolhouses, the schoolmasters and the school curriculum were on the whole decidedly in keeping with the pioneer conditions of the period. The country was being opened up. Settlers were pouring in, many of whom had very little conception of the character of the life to which they were coming. Children as well as parents were absorbed in a struggle with an environment from which, for some years at least, little was to be gained beyond a mere livelihood. It was said more than once in those early days that a farm could be won from "the bush" only at the cost of two generations. The boy of ten years, since he could drive a yoke of oxen, was put to work and hence had little time for further schooling. The winter schools broke up about "sugar-making" time because the children would thereafter be needed at home.

It must be remembered, however, that the comparatively primitive conditions which existed, while they gave little time for the conventional training of the school, also made little demand for it. To be able to handle the axe and the plow was a more necessary accomplishment even than to read, write and cipher. Then again, the majority of the settlers were poor, the Government, as we have seen, was far from liberal in its grants for common schools, the teachers were often most unsuited to their work, both as regards character and equipment, hence much of the "schooling" which the children of the pioneers received could scarcely be dignified with the name of education. It is small wonder, then, that one writer on pioneer life in Upper Canada should inform us that a petition which was sent to the Old Country

Common School—Its Essential Characteristics. 69

in 1828 bore on it seventy-eight thousand X marks,[1] the inference of course being that a very large proportion of the adult male population of the Province at that date were wholly illiterate.

One of the most scholarly of Canadian historians, Dr. Bourinot, finds an excuse for this illiteracy, and its accompanying lack of refinement, in the condition of mind which a solitary life engenders as well as in the hard life of the backwoods which made schooling difficult. He insists also, and rightly, that these defects had certain redeeming virtues associated with them. His remarks are worth quoting at some length.

The isolation of their (i. e. the settlers') lives, he tells us had naturally the effect of making even the better class narrow-minded, selfish, and at last careless of anything like refinement. Men who lived for years without the means of frequent communication with their fellows, without opportunity for social instructive intercourse, except what they might enjoy at rare intervals through the visit of some intelligent clergyman or tourist, might well have little ambition except to gratify the grosser wants of their natures. The post-office, the school and the church were only to be found in the majority of cases at a great distance from their homes. Their children, as likely as not, grew up in ignorance even with educational facilities at hand; for in those days the parent had absolute need of the son's help in the avocations of pioneer life. Yet with all these disadvantages, these men displayed a spirit of manly independence which was in some measure a test of their capacity for better things.[2]

All this is, of course, more or less commonplace, as are also, perhaps, the details which are to follow; yet there is about the persons and things described a certain distinctive element due to distinctive features in the political and social life which formed a background for them. The pioneer school of Upper Canada resembled, it is true, its counterpart in Indiana, Illinois and Kentucky; yet it differed as well.

It would be difficult to find a schoolhouse more primitive than was the one used by the first public school in the County of Victoria. "The schoolhouse, or building used as such, was an old log shanty about twenty by twelve feet, covered with elm bark, a flat roof—it had neither window, floor or fireplace or stove, consequently it could be used only in summer."[3]

The "home-made" character of one of the early schools in Bayham Township extended even to the hinges and the latch

---
[1] Lizars, *In the Days of the Canada Company*, p. 437.
[2] Bourinot, *The Intellectual Development of the Canadian People*, pp. 10, 11.
[3] From the letter of a superannuated school teacher, given in *Doc. Hist.*, Vol. IV, p. 147.

on the door. "The walls were built of logs dovetailed at the corners, the chinks being filled in with mud. Logs formed the rafters, and large pine slabs were used instead of shingles. These latter were weighed down by logs firmly tied to the building by willow withes. Inside, wooden pins were driven part way into the wall and on these pine planks were laid. These planks extended nearly around the building and formed the desks. Half of a bass-wood log, the flat side dressed smooth, was supported by four heavy wooden legs and formed the bench. The door had wooden hinges and a wooden latch. A large fireplace supplied warmth in cold weather."[1]

Of the uncomfortable and unsanitary condition of these early schoolhouses, no special evidence is perhaps necessary, yet the comment of a writer in the *Kingston Gazette* in 1818 is worth quoting both because of its vividness and because of its humor. "One might suppose," this gentleman remarks, "from the shattered condition and ill-accommodation of many schoolhouses, that they were erected as pounds to confine unruly boys and punish them by freezing them and smoking them, so that the master can do little more than regulate the ceremonies of the hearth."

There was no one distinct type of the early schoolmaster, rather, there were several. There was first, the old countryman of decayed fortunes. A specimen of this class is thus described in a letter which Dr. Hodgins includes in his *Documentary History.* "He was an Irishman . . . and a graduate of Trinity College, Dublin. He drifted to Emily (Township) where he took up the land granted to him as a discharged soldier, but, being not used to manual labor, he did not stay long on the land. The settlers, being desirous of getting their children as much of an education as the resources of the country and their own limited means could afford, held a meeting and concluded to endeavor to make an arrangement with Mr. H———— to open a school. The result was that he was engaged to teach while the weather kept fine at the rate of eight dollars per month."[2] This same poor fellow, we are told, later, was found dead in the roadway a few months afterwards, as the result of an over-

---

[1] From "Prize Sketches of Schools in the County of Elgin," published in the *St. Thomas Journal* and reprinted in *Doc. Hist.*, pp. 140-144.
[2] Letter from a superannuated school teacher, *Doc. Hist.*, IV, p. 147.

indulgence in the potent whiskey of the time. Then there was the ambitious young man, who, perhaps, had had the advantage of one or more winters at one of the district grammar schools. Like the college or academy student of New England during this same period, he taught school as a means of livelihood while preparing for a more lucrative or a more honorable calling, such as that of the law, of medicine or of the ministry.

Again, there were some men, though how many it is impossible to tell, who continued in the profession and even in the same school for a considerable number of years and who, both as regards scholarship and character, were worthy of a larger remuneration and more favorable conditions of work than the times afforded. These men were to be found more particularly in the older and more thickly settled districts where the school as an institution had more chance to flourish and where the work of the master was more highly regarded and hence better rewarded than in the newer portions of the Province.

A fourth, and if contemporary accounts are to be accepted, a very numerous class was that of the schoolmaster adventurer of the type of Ichabod Crane and own brother to the hedge-schoolmaster of the South before the war. These wanderers were very frequently Americans and were none the more highly regarded because of that fact. It must be remembered that we are dealing with the period immediately following the War of 1812-1815, and that to the loyal Briton of that day the name "American" had as sinister a meaning as the name "Yankee" had to the Virginian or the Georgian of the decade before the Civil War. All this was narrow-minded of course and yet, with the memory of an American invasion fresh in their minds and with many of the United Empire Loyalists still alive, it was most natural.

We are informed that as early as 1799 it had been the policy of the government " to exclude schoolmasters from the States lest they should instill Republicanism into the tender minds of the youth of the Province."[1] The Reverend John Cosens Ogden, an American clergyman who visited the Province in 1809, records the following as his impressions: " Dreading revolutions, they (the inhabitants) are cautious in receiving Republicans from the

---

[1] Smith, *A Geographical Account of the British Possessions in North America.*

States and wish to encourage husbandmen and laborers only. Clergymen, lawyers, physicians and schoolmasters from the States are not the first characters which would be fostered. Many congregations would be formed and schools opened if the policy in this particular had been different."[1]

Mr. Robert Gourlay in his *Statistical Account of Upper Canada* asserts that nearly four-fifths of the settlers in Upper Canada in 1818 had come from the United States. After making all due allowance for the Loyalist immigration immediately subsequent to the Revolutionary War, it is evident that a great many of these settlers must have come into the Province since 1800. Mr. Gourlay himself refers to the loyalty of these people to Great Britain during the struggle of 1812-1815. It was doubtless the existence in the Province of such a large number of American-born citizens that gave the itinerant American teacher his opportunity, if it did not create an active demand for him. There is abundant evidence that he at least was there and that his presence was looked upon by many with great disfavor. The criticisms offered upon his activity were generally similar in character to the following which is a quotation from a *Statistical Account of Upper Canada* published in 1836.

It is really melancholy to traverse the Province and go into many of the Common Schools; you will find a herd of children instructed by some anti-British adventurer, instilling into their young and tender minds sentiments hostile to the Parent State; false accounts of the late war of 1812, in which Great Britain was engaged with the United States; Geography, setting forth New York, Philadelphia, Boston, etc., as the largest and finest cities in the world; historical reading books describing the American population as the most free and enlightened under Heaven; insisting on the superiority of their laws and institutions to those of all the world; in defiance of the mob supremacy daily witnessed and lamented; and American Spelling Books, Dictionaries and Grammars, teaching them an anti-British dialect and idiom although living in a Province and being subjects of the British Crown.[2]

Practically all the writers on the common schools of the period, and this includes the authors of the various reports of Select Committees of the House of Assembly on Education, agree in several important respects, which may be mentioned here by way of summarizing this especial phase of our subject:

---

[1] *A Tour through Upper and Lower Canada, By a Citizen of the United States*, p. 55.
[2] Dr. Thomas Rolph, *A Statistical Account of Upper Canada.*

Common School—Its Essential Characteristics.   73

(1) They unite in calling attention to the extremely transitory character of the average teacher. "In every township," says Mr. Flindall, in an article from which we have already quoted, "a teacher of twelve months' standing is a prodigy; one of as many weeks the most common."[1] A resolution introduced into the House of Assembly in 1831 speaks of common school teaching as having become "a mere matter of convenience to transitory persons or common idlers who often stay but for one season and leave the schools vacant till they accommodate some other like person."[2]

(2) They are unanimous in emphasizing the total unfitness, both moral and intellectual, of a great many of the common school teachers. Stronger language could scarcely be used than is to be found in reports of the Select Committees just referred to and in resolutions which from time to time received the serious attention of the House of Assembly. One such resolution, for example, speaks of "the youth of the Province being left without due cultivation or, what is still worse, frequently with vulgar, low-bred, vicious and intemperate examples before them in the person of their monitors."[3]

(3) They attribute the low state of the common schools in the main to the meagreness of the Government appropriations. For example, a Select Committee of the House of Assembly in 1833 reports that "these District Common Schools have deteriorated since the reduction of the annual appropriation to their support. . . . In some of the districts not more than four or five pounds can justly be given to any one teacher and, should there be no remedy next year, the grant will admit of only two or three pounds each which would be something like a mockery."[4] A Parliamentary Commission which in 1839 made a careful investigation and an exhaustive report voices the same sentiment in language differing little from the foregoing. They account for the "want either of literary or moral qualifications in the common school teachers" as follows: "The cause of the unfitness your committee believe to be the inadequate remuneration which is held out to those who would embrace this occupa-

---

[1] Essay on Education in Upper Canada published in *Kingston Gazette*, 1818. Reprinted in *Doc. Hist.*, Vol. I, pp. 133–135.
[2] Proceedings of House of Assembly for 1831. In *Doc. Hist.*, Vol. II, p. 51.
[3] *Educational Proceedings of House of Assembly for 1831*, *Doc. Hist.*, Vol. II, p. 51.
[4] Report of Committee, *Doc. Hist.*, Vol. II, p. 109.

tion. In this country, the wages of the working classes are so high that few undertake the office of schoolmaster except those who are unable to do anything else."[1]

The common school curricula of the day were, of course, in keeping with the schoolhouses in which they were taught and with the teachers who administered them. Certainly nothing very extensive could be expected of the first teacher in School Section No. 8, Malahide Township, "who only knew how to read and write a little."[2] Of a somewhat similar character must have been those who qualified for their positions under the Act of 1824, one of whose clauses, as we have seen, stipulated that, in the examination of teachers, "due regard should be had at all times to the degree of education wanting or to the branches necessary to be taught in the township, village or place in which such teacher hath undertaken or is about to teach, a common school."[3]

Very illuminating indeed, in this connection, is the following description of the practices in vogue in the first common schools of what is now one of the most prosperous and enlightened rural communities in the Province. After giving a formidable list of studies "which are the terror of the luckless child of to-day, who has to carry enough of books to make them [sic] tired physically as well as mentally," the writer of the sketch in question remarks, "On starting to school, the child of by-gone days simply had to carry a 'shingle' on which his letters were printed. This he would study until tired when he would quietly raise [sic] up, place his book on the seat and sit down. There being no desks to hold the books, this style of book was very handy as there was no danger of the leaves being torn out."

"After the letters were thoroughly learned, the first step in advance was promotion to the class which was engaged in the study of the New Testament, the Bible being then the standard text-book for reading. The scholars were thoroughly drilled in the teachings of Bible truths for a long time after learning to read fairly well. Not until the scholar could read and spell well was he allowed to begin to write and a good deal of pains was taken to teach the scholar to write well. The pens used

---

[1] From Report of Commission, *Doc. Hist.*, Vol. III, pp. 243–283. The extract given occurs on p. 249.
[2] From "Prize Sketches of Schools in Elgin County"—*Doc. Hist.*, Vol. IV, p. 140.
[3] Sec. VI of Act.

were made of goose quills, the ink also was made of soft maple bark, oak galls or something of that nature. To buy ink was impossible at that time and steel pens had not come into general use. The copy-books were often made of wrapping paper, foolscap paper was very scarce and expensive. A little arithmetic was also taught and this in the majority of cases was the total amount of education which the pupils had the chance to receive. More advanced pupils were taught a little grammar, geography and history."[1]

The following daily program[2] of the York common school in 1821 is of value in this connection as showing: (1) A purely formal course of study consisting of reading, writing, spelling, parsing, analyzing, arithmetic tables, etc.; (2) the use of the New Testament as a text-book, apparently for purposes of "the letter" rather than for those of "the spirit;" (3) the requirement of weekly recitations in the Church Catechism; (4) the segregation of boys and girls in the two lower classes:

All the classes (at least four lessons a day) read, spell and parse.
Examinations are held every evening in Grammar, Spelling and Arithmetic Tables. The Church Catechism is heard once a week. The following is the daily order of studies:

MORNING.

		Books Used.
First Class of Boys.	Grammar Lessons, Exercises on Grammar, Reading, Spelling and Parsing; Writing or Arithmetic.	Murray's English Reader; Murray's Grammar and Exercises; Gray and Walkinghame's Arithmetic.
First Class of Girls.	Grammar "Tasks," Definitions, Correction of Erroneous Syntax; Reading Parsing and Spelling; Writing or Arithmetic.	Enfield's Speaker; Murray's Grammar and Exercises; Carpenter's Scholar's Assistant; Walkinghame's Arithmetic.
Second Class of Boys.	Grammar, Parsing; Etymology, Reading, Spelling and Writing.	New Testament, Murray's Grammar and Spelling Book.
Second Class of Girls.	Grammar Lessons; Definitions, Reading, Spelling and Parsing; Writing.	Barrie's Reader, Murray's Grammar; Carpenter's Assistant; Scott's Lessons; Writing.

[1] *Doc. Hist.*, Vol. I, p. 166, Reprint of articles from the *St. Thomas Journal* on "Schools and Dominies, in the Township of Aldborough."
[2] Given in *Doc. Hist.*, Vol. I, p. 182.

Third and Fourth Class of Children.	Spelling, Reading Analyzing, Orthography.	Testament and Murray's Spelling Book.
	AFTERNOON.	
First Class of Boys.	Reading, Spelling and Parsing; Writing or Arithmetic.	Same as in the morning.
First Class of Girls.	Reading, Spelling and Parsing, Writing and Arithmetic.	Same as in the morning.
Second Class of Boys.	Reading, Spelling, Parsing and Writing.	Same as in the morning.
Second Class of Girls.	Reading, Spelling, Parsing and Writing.	Same as in the morning.
Third and Fourth Classes.	Same as in the morning.	

A very noticeable feature of the social life of the period was the scarcity of books. Mr. Edward Allen Talbot, an educated Englishman who came to the Province in 1818, asserts in one of a series of letters to the Old Country, subsequently collected and published in book form, that during five years' residence in Upper Canada he saw only two persons with books in their hands and that one of these cases was that of a man who was consulting a medical work for a disease with which he was afflicted. "Indeed," Mr. Talbot goes on to say, "the scarcity of books in the country parts of Canada is nearly as great as that of pineapples on the summit of Snowdon."[1] This scarcity, on account of the poverty of many of the settlers and on account also of the absence of suitable depots for distribution, extended even to school books. It was this condition of affairs doubtless which led to the provision of the Act of 1816 authorizing District Boards of Education to expend certain amounts in the purchase of text-books and to distribute those books as circumstances might demand. This permissive legislation seems to have availed little however, since throughout the entire period under consideration the lack of satisfactory text-books was a fruitful source of complaint.

In the first school established at Richmond Hill in the Home District (in 1820) there was evidently not only a lacking of

---

[1] From Letter XXX of the series, quoted in *Doc. Hist.*, Vol. I, pp. 194-196.

books but also a lack of uniformity in what few there were. Of this school we are told: " The books, all sorts and sizes—home supplies—were few and far between and were shoved along the class until each scholar got his share of the lesson. The first passable supply of books of instruction that arrived in our village was imported from the British and Foreign Bible Society in England."[1]

Most of the books used in the common schools at this time seem to have been American publications, works whose anti-British character has been referred to in another connection. Notwithstanding the fact that the dangers involved in such a practice were recognized at least as early as 1822,[2] for more than twenty years no adequate effort was made to provide school books more acceptable from the patriotic standpoint. The Parliamentary Commission of 1839 was able to report as follows: " Your commission regret to find that editions published in the United States are much used throughout the Province; tinctured as they are by principles which, however fit for dissemination under the form of Government which exists there, cannot be inculcated here without evil results."[3] In fact it was not till 1850 that a system of text-books was adopted and an enactment made forbidding the use of " any foreign book in the English branches in any Common or Model School without the express permission of the Council of Public Instruction."[4] It may be remarked here that by both the Acts of 1843 and 1850 American teachers were excluded from the schools until they had taken the oath of naturalization.

Some feeble attempts were, however, apparently made to meet the deficiency in the matter of text-books. In the minutes of the General Board of Education for May 6th, 1828, there is the following entry:

The Board met this day and after discussing the matter it was: Resolved that the Mavor's English Spelling Book, reprinted at Kingston by Mr. James McFarlane, is a Book which it would be desirable to introduce into the Common Schools throughout this Province; and that in order to do so with the least expense, and so as to afford the necessary number of copies, it is advisable to have the work printed on paste-board sheets, containing a page on each side of the sheet.

[1] From a private letter printed in *Doc. Hist.*, Vol. II, p. 154.
[2] See letter of Lt. Gov. Sir Peregrine Maitland to Earl Bathurst in *Doc. Hist.*, Vol. III, p. 3.
[3] Report of Parl. Com. on Ed., 1839, *Doc. Hist.*, Vol. III, p. 250.
[4] 13th Victoria, Chap. 48, Sec. 14, "An Act for the better establishment and maintenance of Common Schools in Upper Canada.

The President was requested to ascertain what the charge will be of printing the work in this form and what would be the expense of 2000 copies. It was also: Resolved that the expense be ascertained of printing, in the same form, such a small elementary treatise in arithmetic, as the President shall think eligible for the use of the Common Schools.[1]

The unfortunate condition of the Province as regards school buildings, school teachers and school equipment, which has been described in the foregoing, was no doubt due at the outset to a widespread apathy in regard to public elementary education but for the continuance of these conditions throughout so long a period the small group of public officials in whose hands political power was concentrated, were mainly responsible. Their chief interest was elsewhere than in the common schools. They tried, as was said by one of the critics of the time, to construct their educational pyramid from the apex downward. Failure was, of course, inevitable but that failure made possible a reconstruction along broader lines. That this reconstruction is still in progress, is evident to any careful student of educational conditions in the Province of Ontario at the present time.

[1] *Doc. Hist.*, Vol. III, p. 3.

CHAPTER VII.

THE RELIGIOUS FACTOR IN PUBLIC EDUCATION—THE GRAMMAR AND THE COMMON SCHOOLS.

A study of the present educational crisis in England is exceedingly instructive to a student of the relationships which have existed historically between religion and the schools. It reveals the fact that there is in the politics of that country an influential element who desire a continuance of the ascendancy of the Church of England in elementary education. It shows also that there is another and a much stronger element numerically, who, while they believe in religious instruction in the schools, yet desire to make full concession to the " non-conformist conscience." Just such a condition existed in Upper Canada in the early part of the nineteenth century. There was practically a unanimity of sentiment in favor of the union of religious with secular education but there were serious differences of opinion in regard to the specific form which the religious element was to assume.

Naturally, those who upheld the theory that the Church of England was as definitely the Established Church of Upper Canada as it was of the mother country—notably Dr. (afterwards Bishop) Strachan—believed that public education in all its stages should be controlled by that Church. Just as naturally, the leaders in the other denominations, since they were opposed to the claims of the Church of England to a sole right to the enjoyment of the public land set apart for " a Protestant clergy," were equally emphatic in denying the right of that Church to supreme control of public education in the Province. What was sought by these men was a division of power and a form of religious instruction which did not carry on its surface the hall-mark of any particular creed.

We have alluded already (in Chapter V) to the concessions made in the School Act of 1841 to the Roman Catholic Church. That religious body believed then, as it believes now, that formal instruction in religion should be given along with the instruction in the so-called secular branches of learning. It emphasized the serious dangers which threaten when the former is relegated to a separate period and to a separate class of instructors. As a result of this view and of the various legislative provisions which subsequently amplified and continued the privileges granted by the Act of 1841, formal instruction in Roman Catholic dogma occupies a prominent place in the curriculum of every separate school in the Province of Ontario at the present time. Of *every* separate school since, so far as the present writer is aware, at least, no Protestant denomination has availed itself of the privilege, which is granted to it by law, of establishing special public schools for the children of its communion.

The Protestant denominations, throughout the whole history of the Province, while they have believed in religious instruction in the public schools, have naturally had, because of important differences in creed, considerable difficulty in agreeing as to the exact matter of the instruction. Eventually, however, a sort of tacit agreement has been arrived at which confines the religious exercises of the school to the daily reading of the Bible, without comment by the teacher, and the daily recitation of a formal prayer. In the early grammar and common schools, however, the religious instruction given was much more direct and extensive.

We have already referred to the attacks which were made on the grammar schools on the ground that they ministered solely to the needs of a wealthy and aristocratic class. Other and equally strenuous objections were made to them on the ground that they were in reality establishments of the Church of England. This objection received its most elaborate statement in a petition of the United Presbytery of Upper Canada to the House of Assembly in January, 1830.[1] Certain paragraphs of this petition are of sufficient importance to be given in their entirety; they read as follows:

> From the manner in which your petitioners in their ministerial capacity, stand connected with a very large portion of His Majesty's subjects in this Province, they have the means of knowing and it is with deep regret they are compelled to say that the state of education is in general, in a deplorable condition.
>
> Although for many years, a liberal provision has been made for the education of the youth in this Province, the benevolent designs of the Legislature have failed in effecting the object they had in view.

---

[1] Copy of Petition, *Doc. Hist.*, Vol. I, pp. 298, 299.

The Religious Factor in Public Education. 81

The appointment of trustees from one communion alone has occasioned a jealousy in the minds of the people and destroyed that confidence which should ever be placed in the public institutions of our country.

It might have been expected that, as all classes of the community and all denominations of Christians have to bear the expenses of these institutions, the interests of all would have been consulted, and that persons of intelligence in all denominations would have been allowed to participate in their superintendence.

Your Petitioners with deep regret find that this is not the case; and that the Trustees of these institutions, which ought to be impartially managed for the benefit of all, have been almost exclusively appointed from one denomination of Christians, and consequently, your Petitioners and their congregations, as well as others in similar circumstances, have been deprived of that benefit which they had a right to expect would have arisen from them.

Your Petitioners having numerous and large congregations under their superintendence, in which there are thousands of young people growing up in want of education, feel anxious that they should be provided with the means of instruction which would render them intelligent Christians and useful members of society.

As these institutions are now managed, your Petitioners have no alternative left but to apply to your Honorable House to afford them provision for other Schools to be placed under their superintendence, since they are not permitted to have any share in the appointment of Teachers or in the management of the District (Grammar) Schools now in existence.

When the petition reached the Legislative Council, a committee of that body was appointed to investigate the questions raised. The report of this committee[1] contained a denial in toto of the charges made by the Presbytery. " For these allegations," so the report reads, " your committee, after the minutest enquiry, have discovered that there is not the slightest foundation, and they think it a matter much to be regretted, that a body of men acting under so respectable a name as ' The United Presbytery of Upper Canada' should have advanced statements so entirely unsupported by facts." The Act of 1807 which established the grammar schools, the committee says in substance, made " fitness, discretion, moral character, learning and capacity " the only necessary qualifications of the trustees to be appointed for these schools. The first District Boards of Trustees constituted under the act contained Roman Catholics and Presbyterians as well as Anglicans. In fact, in the Newcastle

---
[1] In *Doc. Hist.*, Vol. I, pp. 307-310.

District, only one of the trustees was a member of the Church of England.

Even if the trustees were all Anglicans, the committee insists, such a fact would not make the schools sectarian if fitness and character were made the sole tests in the appointment of teachers. Then follows a list of the grammar school teachers from 1807 till that time, with a statement of their church affiliations. The list as given includes twenty Anglican teachers and eighteen of other religious persuasions, sixteen of whom are mentioned as Presbyterians and "six in holy orders." A noticeable fact, but one to which the committee does not call attention, is that thirteen of the Anglican teachers are clergymen.

The "argumentum ad hominem" is introduced in the assertion "that, on the occasion of a vacancy in the District of Johnstown, the Reverend William Smart, the very gentleman who in the capacity of moderator of the Presbyterians, signs the petition referred to us, might have obtained the situation of Teacher of the District School of that District, in which he then resided and still resides, and that he declined undertaking the charge."

The Presbytery, in returning to the attack,[1] called attention to the following facts:

(1) That Legislative Council in its reply begs the question at issue. It confines itself to a description of the character of the original district trustees. It does not offer any evidence to show that the trustees of 1830 are not of the character alleged in the petition.

(2) That though the Act of 1807 was unsectarian in nature, the grammar schools established under it have since come under sectarian control; hence there is the greater cause for complaint.

(3) Instead of refuting the charges of the Presbytery by giving the names of the present trustees with a statement of their church affiliations, the committee in question confines itself to compiling a list of grammar school masters and noticing that they have not all been of the Church of England. "But if this proves anything, it proves too much, for they have thus unintentionally given us additional proof of the exclusive system that has been pursued. For of those teachers that were not originally Episcopalians before they came under the influence of

---

[1] In Report of a Committee, June 1, 1830, given in *Doc. Hist.*, Vol. I, pp. 315–316.

this exclusive system, it is a remarkable fact and one deserving of particular notice, that many have (to use their own words), ' Since that taken orders in the Church of England.' "

(4) Finally, it is a matter of personal knowledge with the members of the Presbytery "that the Trustees of the District Schools are almost exclusively appointed from one religious denomination, and that they are not aware that a single clergyman of any denomination other than the Church of England has ever been appointed Trustee of the District (Grammar) Schools or that any clergyman of the Church of England resident in the town or village where the District (Grammar) School is established has been passed by."

The controversy which has just been described illustrates the great difficulty of apportioning political authority among rival religious denominations in such a way that each shall feel that it has received its just share. It also shows that whether the grammar schools of the time were sectarian institutions or not they were at least regarded as such by a large proportion of the inhabitants of the Province. This feeling was intensified rather than diminished by the organization of Upper Canada College, the " superior grammar school " or " minor college " founded by Sir John Colborne in 1829. The principal and five of the masters of this school were clergymen of the Church of England and to that communion belonged also the Visitor and the Governing Board.

The opposition of the Presbyterians and the Methodists expressed itself in movements for the establishment of schools which should, in a measure at least, parallel the work of Upper Canada College. As early as 1830, the United Presbytery had considered the advisability of a " Literary Institution, embracing a course of appropriate studies for those who are assigned for the Christian ministry,"[1] and of an appeal to the Provincial Government and to the general public for aid in the enterprise. In 1831, such a public appeal was made and funds were solicited in the United States as well as in Canada.

Further action, looking towards the erection of buildings, was taken in 1832.[2] The activity of the church in this connection

---
[1] From minutes of meeting of Presbytery, Jan. 11, 1830, quoted from *Brockville Recorder* of Jan., 1830, in *Doc. Hist.*, Vol. I, p. 315.
[2] Dr. Gregg, *Hist. of Presbyterian Church in Canada*, pp. 444-445.

was, it would seem, for several years, intermittent, and hence without definite result. Finally, however, in 1840, a Presbyterian school known as Queen's College was established at Kingston. Since many of the circumstances attending the establishment of this institution had a direct connection with the question of a Provincial university, any statement of them may properly be assigned to the following chapter.

The protest of the Methodists against Executive partiality took definite shape much more quickly than did that of the Presbyterians. A conference held in 1830 resolved to proceed at once to the founding of "a Seminary of Learning to be under the control of the Methodist Episcopal Church."[1] The site of this Seminary was, shortly afterwards fixed at Cobourg. Its constitution, and in this respect it differed radically from the school projected by the Presbyterians, made it "a purely Literary Institution." "No system of Divinity shall be taught therein but all students shall be free to embrace and pursue any religious creed and attend any place of religious worship which their parents or guardians may direct."[2]

This academy received a Royal Charter in May, 1836, and was formally opened on the eighteenth of the following month. A prospectus prepared in that year and printed for circulation in England in connection with an appeal for funds mentions the following as "the specific objects of the institution." "(1) To educate upon terms equally moderate with similar institutions in the neighboring republic of the United States, and with strict attention to their morals, youth of Canada generally. (2) To educate for Common School Teachers free of charge, poor young men of Christian principles and character, and of promising talents, who have an ardent thirst for knowledge. (3) To educate the most promising youth of the recently converted Indian tribes of Canada, as Teachers to their aboriginal countrymen."[3]

A patriotic reason for a generous support of the school existed in the fact that "For want of such an institution, upwards of sixty of the youth of Canada are now attending Seminaries of Learning, under a similar management in the United States, where nearly two hundred Canadian youth have been taught

[1] *Doc. Hist.*, Vol. II, p. 2.
[2] Copy of Charter, *Doc. Hist.*, Vol. II, pp. 268-272.
[3] *Doc. Hist.* Vol. II, p. 241.

the elementary branches of a professional education during the last eight years. There is good reason that nearly, if not quite, all the Canadian youth now being taught in the United States Seminaries of Learning will return to Canada as soon as this Institution shall have been brought into operation; besides the attendance of other Canadian youth, some of whom have been kept at home by their parents, for several months past, awaiting the opening of this Institution."[1]

The academy at the outset gave instruction in the purely elementary subjects as well as in such higher branches as Latin, Greek, Hebrew, Mathematics and the Natural Sciences. So successful was the school and so skillfully were its affairs administered that, in 1841, it was, by an act of the Legislature of the United Provinces, enlarged into a college, named from the then reigning queen of England, Victoria College.

That the Upper Canada Academy was, in a sense, a protest against the exclusiveness which characterized Upper Canada College, as regards both its administration and its curriculum, is evident to any one who compares the two institutions in these particulars. That the founder of Upper Canada College, Sir John Colborne, saw in the projected Academy a rival to his own school, and appreciated the chief reasons for the activity of the Methodists in thus establishing a school of their own, appears quite clearly from a letter[2] which he sent, in 1831, to a Methodist Conference which was then in session. This letter was in acknowledgment of the receipt of certain memorials which the Conference had asked him to forward to His Majesty and of certain expressions of good will which had been addressed to him personally. In it, the Lieutenant-Governor censured the Conference and the church it represented in decidedly undiplomatic language for their lack of sympathy with the political and educational policies of the administration. He informed them that "a very unfavorable impression had been made from one end of the Province to the other as regards an imported secular interference on the part of (their) preachers." He insinuated that the Methodist ministers took advantage "of the influence acquired by their sacred office to conduct the political concerns of the people committed to their care to be instructed

[1] *Doc. Hist.*, Vol. II, p. 241.
[2] Copy of letter, *Doc. Hist.*, Vol. II, pp. 11-12.

only in the word of life." With a manifest reference to the plans for a Methodist Academy then under consideration, he remarked, " The System of Education which has produced the best and ablest men in the United Kingdom will not be abandoned here to suit the limited views of the leaders of societies who perhaps have neither experience or judgment to appreciate the value or advantages of a liberal education. A Seminary, I hope will not be styled exclusive that is open to everyone, merely because its classical masters are brought from our own universities."

The reply to this communication, undertaken on behalf of the Conference by the Reverend Egerton Ryerson, defended the Methodist ministers against the charges of unpatriotic behavior and pernicious political activity and asserted that the opposition to Upper Canada College was not because its masters were brought from the British universities but because the College itself " was established and placed under the control of one Church without even consulting the popular branch of the Colonial Legislature."[1]

When we turn to a consideration of common school education we find even a stronger instance of Executive arrogance and ecclesiastical domination than existed in the case of Upper Canada College. The instance in question is that of the Church of England " National " School which was established at York in 1820 through the efforts of the Reverend Doctor Strachan. This school was supported for over twenty years partly from the university endowment and partly from the Provincial revenues. A complete system of " National " schools, which was eventually to absorb the whole work of elementary instruction in the Province, was planned at this time but only one other school of the class—that at Peterborough—was actually put into operation. The only record that can be found of this latter school, so far as the present writer is aware, consists in a few scattered references in the Legislative documents of the time to an annual grant of some sixty pounds to its support.

A definite though rather tardy attempt was made in 1822 to secure the Royal approval of the plan which has just been outlined. In 1822, the Lieutenant-Governor, Sir Peregrine Mait-

---

[1]From portion of letter quoted in *Doc. Hist.*, Vol. II, p. 12.

land, submitted to the Colonial Secretary, Earl Bathurst, a scheme of popular elementary education involving " an introductory school on the National plan in each town of a certain size." The number of these schools was to be increased " as the circumstances of the Province may require and the means allow."[1] This application of the Lieutenant-Governor, was of course in reality a request for the Royal endorsement of a policy which had been in operation—in part at least—for some two years.

The Colonial Secretary, in a reply dated October 12th, 1823, conveyed His Majesty's consent to an appropriation of " a portion of the Reserves set apart for the establishment of a university, for the support of Schools on the National plan of Education."[2]

The reader is doubtless acquainted with the educational movement which took place in England in the early part of the nineteenth century and which is associated with the names of Dr. Andrew Bell and Mr. Joseph Lancaster. He has, doubtless, also some knowledge of the chief feature of the two " systems "— the employment of the more advanced pupils in the school as teachers of the less advanced, and the consequent material cheapening of the cost of elementary instruction.

Both the Bell and the Lancaster systems found their way into Upper Canada. The former was employed as has been mentioned. The latter was adopted in 1815 by an organization known as " The Midland District School Society." Though the work of this society was not without educational significance, it was not in any way under public control; neither did it receive public aid, hence the Lancasterian schools which it conducted do not properly fall within the province of this study.

The local circumstances attending the establishment of the Central National School at York are rather complicated but the essential facts appear to be as follows: In 1820 a Mr. Thomas Appleton was the teacher of the common school at York and was regarded by the trustees and by the community at large as highly successful in his work. When by the School Act of that year, the annual legislative grant for schools was reduced from £6,000 to £2,500, the Board of Education for the Home District instead of making a proportionate reduction in the

---
[1] Quoted in *Doc. Hist.*, Vol. I, p. 179.
[2] *Ibid.*

allowance to each school within its jurisdiction, arbitrarily discontinued the grant to Mr. Appleton. The chairman of the District Board, Dr. Strachan, had, it appears, asked some time before for the use of the school building for a school on the "National" pattern to be placed in charge of a teacher to be sent out by the Central National School at London. This request had been refused by the trustees on the ground that to grant it would involve, on their part, a breach of faith with Mr. Appleton. When, a few month afterwards, the Provincial grant was cut off from the school, it was felt both by Mr. Appleton and the trustees to be an act of retaliation on the part of Dr. Strachan and the other members of the District Board of Education. These gentlemen of course justified their action on grounds of economy. A "National" school being projected for York, there was no further need of the public common school and the money withheld from Mr. Appleton could very advantageously be used in increasing the grants to the other common schools of the District.

A further stage in the controversy was reached when, in September, 1820, by the direction of the Lieutenant-Governor, the school building, then vacant, was appropriated for the purposes of a "National" school and a Mr. Joseph Spragge installed as teacher. The arbitrary nature of this proceeding appears in all the stronger light when one remembers that the building in question was erected with funds obtained by popular subscription for the express purpose of carrying into effect the provisions of the Common School Act of 1816.

Of the character of the "National" plan of education as exemplified in his school, Mr. Spragge later testified before a committee of the House of Assembly that he used the Rev. Dr. Bell's system which he considered as prior in invention to Mr. Lancaster's and that the principal difference between the two systems was that "Dr. Bell's system is in accordance with the Established Church and in my school I use the Church Catechism and a Collect at morning and evening prayer. But the children are not taught the Church Catechism when their parents object to it."[1]

In the meantime, Mr. Appleton continued teaching at York, though without any support other than the fees of his pupils.

---
[1] Evidence before Committee of the House of Assembly 1828, in *Doc. Hist.*, Vol. I p. 252.

He carried a claim for redress first to the District Board of Education and later to the Lieutenant-Governor. From these quarters he received no encouragement. Finally, in 1828, he addressed a petition to the House of Assembly on the matter. The House appointed a committee to look into the case. This committee called several witnesses, among them Mr. Appleton himself, Mr. Spragge and the three common school trustees who had contracted for Mr. Appleton's services in 1820. The report which was the outcome of the investigations of this committee recognized the justice of Mr. Appleton's claim and condemned in unequivocal terms the action of the Executive and the District Board of Education. The more significant passages of the Report are as follows:

Your Committee . . . report it, as a matter of regret, that tried and faithful teachers who had devoted themselves to the occupation for years, and were looking forward to it as the labor of their lives, should be superseded by the erection of what is termed a "National" school, which is neither needed by the state of the country, nor the extent of the population.

This "National School" it appears has been supported out of the revenues of the Province without the knowledge and consent of Parliament.

Mr. Spragg, as Teacher of the "Central School" receives £250 per annum, which, with the contingent and other expenses advanced out of the revenues of the Province, amounts to about £300, and the average number of scholars, every year, from its institution to the present time, has been sixty-three.

Upon examining the progress made by some of the children in this Central National School and comparing it with the progress made by others in the Common Schools, in a far shorter time, your Committee find that the latter have made a far greater proficiency.

If the sum appropriated to the "Central School" were distributed as an encouragement to schools in the interior of the country, where money is scarce, and the patronage both needed and deserved, it would be most beneficially felt in every township in the Home District and in every other District in the Province also.

The "National School" is founded upon the Rev. Dr. Bell's system and is professedly adherent to the Church of England—and, therefore, ought not to be supported by the revenues of a country struggling against ecclesiastical exclusion (exclusiveness?).[1]

It does indeed seem a most arbitrary and extravagant piece of behavior that a common school conducted in a building erected by popular subscription should be discontinued on the ground of the insufficiency of the government grant, and that in its place

[1] *Doc. Hist.*, Vol. I, pp. 246-247.

a school of sectarian character should be established by executive mandate and maintained at an expense nearly ten times as great as that of the one which it supplanted.

The "Appleton case," as it was known, dragged along till 1835. In that year the Select Committee of the House of Assembly on Grievances recommended " that £85, 4s. be paid to Mr. Thomas Appleton, Teacher of the Common School of this place in the years 1822, 1823, 1824, 1825, 1826 and 1827, for Public Moneys due to him and withheld by the Board of Education and for the interest thereon accruing."[1]

In the following year Mr. Appleton's claim was again considered in Committee but nothing apparently came of it. The responsibility for the non-payment of the claim, rested, it would seem, with the Executive rather than with the House of Assembly.

The Central National School at York, with Mr. Spragge still at its head, continued into the new régime. As late as 1843 it appears in a Report to the Legislative Assembly by the Provincial Secretary of the educational institutions receiving grants of public money. In 1844, however, because of the organization of a city school system in York (then Toronto), it was discontinued by an order of the Governor-General in Council. At that time, according to a representation made by Mr. Spragge there were three hundred and ninety-six children in attendance at the school.

The plan of Sir Peregrine Maitland and the General Board of Education at the outset seems to have been to make the school at York a training-centre, similar to its prototype in London, where teachers should be prepared for taking charge of the projected National schools throughout the Province. This expectation was, however, never realized, doubtless because of the hostile public sentiment which found expression in the House of Assembly in the Report on the Appleton Case and in other reports to which reference has been made in preceding chapters. The Appleton Case was, however, but one phase of a struggle against ecclesiastical denomination. Another and still more important phase was the agitation which was carried on for many years against the projected establishment of a Provincial University under Church control. This agitation will form the chief subject of the following chapter.

---

[1] *Doc. Hist.*, Vol. II, p. 170.

CHAPTER VIII.

THE RELIGIOUS FACTOR IN PUBLIC EDUCATION—THE PROVINCIAL UNIVERSITY.

An account has already been given of the various events from 1797 onward connected with the provision of a land endowment for a Provincial University in Upper Canada. Mention has also been made of the fact that until 1843 the University as a body of teachers and students did not exist. There remains yet to be described the various university charters and acts and the controversies which arose because of the effort of one portion of the community to secure for the University a distinctly ecclesiastical and Anglican character and the equally persistent endeavor of another element to purge it of all sectarian taint.

The foremost champion of the ecclesiastical party was, of course, the Reverend Dr. Strachan. His views were in the main endorsed and his efforts warmly seconded by the different Lieutenant-Governors of the Province. On his side were ranged also the members of the Legislative Council, who represented, as has been shown, the conservative and artistocratic element in the population. The opposite party, so far as its religious complexion was concerned, was made up of the different dissenting denominations. Its views found expression in the deliberations and resolutions of the House of Assembly. In several instances the House undertook to embody these views in bills; these, while they manifestly expressed the popular will, failed of course, to secure the approval of the Upper House. Such a condition of affairs naturally led to recriminations between the two legislative bodies and to appeals on the part of the House of Assembly to the Royal authority as represented in the Colonial Office. All these facts will appear from the detailed descriptions which follow.

Although the need of a university had been agitated intermittently since 1800, it was not till 1826 that the financial prospects of the institution were felt to be such as to warrant the application for a Royal Charter. In April of that year, the Reverend Dr. Strachan arrived in England charged with the triple mission of effecting an exchange of the unproductive university lands for the more valuable Crown Reserves, of arousing British sympathy and obtaining private aid for the university and of securing the charter in question.

During the early part of his stay in England, Dr. Strachan drew up "An Appeal to the Friends of Religion and Literature in behalf of the University in Upper Canada." In this " appeal " he reviewed the existing school system of the Province, emphasized the need of a school of a higher order which should provide instruction in Law, Medicine and Divinity and called attention to the dangers which threatened from the sending of many Canadian youth to colleges in the United States. He laid especial stress on the needs of the Church. "What can twenty-four clergymen do?" he asked, " scattered over a country of nearly six hundred miles in length? Can we be surprised that, under such circumstances, the religious benefits of a church establishment are unknown, and that sectaries of all descriptions have increased? And when it is further considered that the religious teachers of all other Protestant denominations, a very few respectable ministers of the Church of Scotland excepted, come from the republican states of America, where they gather their knowledge and form their sentiments, it is evident that, if the Imperial Government does not step forward with efficient help, the mass of the population will be gradually nurtured and instructed in hostility to our institutions, both civil and religious."[1] In the concluding paragraph of the " Appeal " he returned to the same theme. " It is chiefly on religious grounds," he insists, " that this Appeal for the University of Upper Canada is made, which, while it offers its benefits to the population, will, for a century to come, from the peculiar circumstances of the country be essentially a Missionary College, and the number of clergymen, which it will be called upon to furnish will be more than double what any other profession can require."[2]

As a result of the efforts of Dr. Strachan, a Royal Charter was granted in 1827. The chief provisions of this charter were as follows:

(1) The Anglican Bishop of the Diocese in which the College might be situated was to be the official visitor of the institution.

---

[1] *Doc. Hist.*, Vol. I, p. 217.
[2] *Ibid*, p. 218.

(2) The Lieutenant-Governor for the time being should be the Chancellor.

(3) The Archdeacon of York should be, ex-officio, the President.

(4) The immediate government of the institution should be in the hands of a Council consisting of the Chancellor, the President and seven of the Professors. These latter were to be members of the Church of England and were required, before their admission to the Council, to subscribe to the Thirty-nine Articles. Prior to the opening of the University, others might be appointed in the place of the professors mentioned, provided that they also met the prescribed religious tests.

(5) No religious tests should be required of any student except of those in Divinity.

It is worthy of note in this connection that Dr. Strachan himself doubted the wisdom of two of the restrictions imposed, viz., the one making the Archdeacon of York President by virtue of his office, and the one requiring subscription of the Professors who should be admitted to the College Council to the Thirty-nine Articles. The Archbishop of Canterbury who was consulted in the matter had, however, no such scruples. On the contrary, he " doubted the propriety of assenting to an instrument so free and comprehensive in its provisions."[1]

As may easily be imagined, the University Charter of 1827 gave serious offense to the House of Assembly. The session of that body which met in 1828 took up the matter in detail. A specific occasion for its activity was found at the outset in the " Petition of Mr. Bulkley Waters and 219 others of different denominations of Christians in the counties of Lennox and Addington praying the House to enquire into the principle upon which an university is to be established in this Province so that no power to hold lands or other property be granted to nor any addition to the number of members composing the House of Assembly be made from, or out of, any ecclesiastical or literary body corporate at whose hands danger could, or might, be apprehended to the Constitution or to their religious liberties."[2] Later in the session other petitions expressing the

---
[1] *Proc. at the Opening of Kings Coll.*, 1843, p. 39.
[2] Ed. Proc. of House of Assembly for 1828, *Doc. Hist.*, Vol. I, p. 234.

same sentiments and signed by some six thousand persons in all, were presented to the House.

These petitions were referred to a select committee and this committee in connection with its report to the House presented the draft of a petition to the King. This petition which was afterwards forwarded to His Majesty, asked for a cancellation of the charter on the ground that "it contains provisions which are calculated to render the institution subservient to the particular interests of that Church (i. e. the Church of England) and to exclude from its offices and honours all who do not belong to it."[1]

"In consequence of these provisions," the petition further states, "its benefits will be confined to a favoured few, while others of Your Majesty's subjects, far more numerous, and equally loyal and deserving of Your Majesty's parental care and favour, will be shut out from a participation in them. Having a tendency to build up one particular church to the prejudice of others, it (i. e. the University) will naturally be an object of jealousy and disgust. Its influence as a Seminary of Learning will, upon these accounts, be limited and partial."[2]

The House, in 1829, passed a series of resolutions which reiterated the chief facts contained in the Report and Petition of the preceding session. In the same year the Legislative Council rejected a resolution of one of its committees which expressed disapproval of the clause in the charter which made the Archdeacon of York, ex-officio, the President of the College. At the same time, however, the Council pronounced in favor of the removal of the religious test for members of the College Council.

The popular discontent with the charter received a fresh expression in 1830 in a petition to the Imperial Parliament from a number of the citizens of York County styling themselves "The Friends of Religious Liberty." This petition was later circulated throughout the Province and received upwards of ten thousand signatures. As the name assumed by its chief promoters would signify, it expressed itself in favor of "an equality of privileges and immunities among all Christian denominations and a system of education under the control of the Provincial Legislature with Schools and Colleges in which there

[1]Ed. Proc. of House of Assembly for 1828, in *Doc. Hist.*, Vol. I, p. 242.
[2]*Ibid.*

should be no preference of sectarian tenets or interests, and whose portals and honours would be equally accessible to meritorious industry of every religious creed."[1]

The agitation in the House of Assembly against the restrictive features of the charter was practically continuous up to 1837. In fact, in 1835, and again in 1836, the House went so far as to express its own views as to the organization and government of a university, in Charter Amendment bills. The Legislative Council in rejecting these bills expressed in quite emphatic language their opinion as to their character. A clause which provided " That no religious test or qualification whatever shall be required of any Chancellor, President, Professor, Tutor, Lecturer, Scholar or other person being a candidate for any situation or honour in the said College " is thus characterized, " By Section Twenty-six, Christianity appears proscribed with a virulence not unworthy of Diocletian. . . . There is not a College or University either in Europe or America or indeed in any part of the world (even not excepting the London University, which has been forced to provide in some degree for religious instruction) without a religious character."[2]

During the period under consideration (1827-1837) the sympathies of the Imperial House of Commons were manifestly with the liberal attitude taken by their Canadian counterpart. In 1828, a committee of that body, to whom had been referred the petition of the House of Assembly of that same year, gave expression to the following opinions: (1) " That with respect to the President, Professors and all others connected with the College, no religious tests should be required." (2) " That in the selection of Professors no rule should be followed and no other object sought than the nomination of the most learned and discreet person. . . . "[3]

The petition from Upper Canada had, it would appear, an effect upon the Colonial Office also. Sir John Colborne, who assumed office as Lieutenant-Governor towards the close of the year 1828, had apparently positive instructions to check the activities, then under way, looking towards the erection of college buildings, until the charter difficulty had been settled. At least,

[1] Copy of Petition, *Doc. Hist.*, Vol. I, p. 318.
[2] Copy of Report of Committee, *Doc. Hist.*, Vol. II, pp. 341-342.
[3] *Doc. Hist.*, Vol. I, pp. 254-255.

the Council of King's College, in 1832, in alluding to a communication made by him to them shortly after his arrival in the Province, was able to remind him that he "declared that 'one stone should not be put upon another' until certain alterations in the charter had been made or proposed to the Legislature, and that as Chancellor, Your Excellency would utterly refuse to concur in any further measures of the Council under present circumstances."[1]

In 1831, the Colonial Office went still further and asked for the surrender of the College Charter and of all funds in the hands of the College Council, with the express understanding, however, that those funds, while in the hands of the Colonial Office, were not to be used for any purpose other than the original one. The reply of the Council to this request is thus referred to by its President, Dr. Strachan, in an address made some ten years later.

> In an able Report the College Council stated their reason for refusing compliance with this extraordinary request and that they did not think it right to concur in surrendering the charter of King's College or its endowment. The College Council further observed, that they did not feel nor profess to feel a sufficient assurance, that after they had consented to destroy a College founded by their Sovereign under as unrestricted and open a charter as had ever passed the Great Seal of England for a similar purpose, the different branches of the Legislature would be able to concur in establishing another that would equally secure to the inhabitants of the colony through successive generations, the possession of a seat of learning in which sound religious instruction should be dispensed and at which care should be taken to guard against those occasions of instability, dissension and confusion, the foresight of which had led in our present state to the making an uniformity in religion in each university throughout the empire an indispensable feature of its constitution.[2]

The Colonial Secretary, not feeling justified in attempting coercion in the matter, contented himself with notifying the Provincial Legislature that when the two houses should agree upon an amended charter His Majesty would consider it favorably. It was not till 1837, however, that the two legislative bodies were able to come to an agreement and even then, the Legislative Council passed the Charter Amendment bill of that year in a very unwilling spirit. It was only because of their

---
[1] Address to Sir John Colborne, from the Council of King's College, March, 1832, given in *Doc. Hist.*, Vol. III, pp. 32–37.
[2] Address at the opening of King's College, 1843—In *Doc. Hist.*, Vol. II, p. 215.

aversion to an indefinite postponement of the founding of the university that they consented to the bill at all. The following were the chief provisions of the measure in question:

(1) The Judges of King's Bench were made the official visitors of the institution.

(2) The President was to be appointed by the King and did not need to be the incumbent of any ecclesiastical office.

(3) The College Council was to be composed of the Chancellor and President of the University, the Speakers of the two Houses of Parliament, the Solicitor and Attorney-General for the time being, the five senior Professors and the Principal of Upper Canada College.

(4) Upper Canada College was incorporated with King's College and placed under the control of the College Council.

(5) A relative, though not an absolute freedom from religious tests was granted by the enactment that "It shall not be necessary that any member of the College Council . . . or any professor to be at any time appointed shall be a member of the Church of England, or subscribe to any articles of religion other than a declaration that they believe in the authenticity and divine inspiration of the Old and New Testaments and in the doctrine of the Trinity."[1]

A point in connection with the amendment of the College Charter and one which occasioned considerable controversy was the matter of the Professorship of Theology. In a Missionary College of the Church of England such as that provided by the Charter of 1827, manifestly only one type of Theology was in place. The Anglican Professorship in Theology was left undisturbed by the Act of 1837. But the Church of Scotland was an established church in Great Britain and hence had some right to recognition as such in the colonies. The Law Officers of the Crown had already pronounced in favor of the claim of that church to a participation in the Clergy Reserves. It was natural then, that the leaders of that church in Upper Canada should go further and insist on their right to a Chair of Presbyterian Theology in the Provincial University. In 1828, the Select Committee of the Imperial House of Commons of which

---

[1] *7th William IV*, Chap. XVI.

mention has already been made, suggested the establishment of such a professorship. In 1831, the United Presbytery of Upper Canada took up the matter in a resolution "That a respectful and immediate application be made to His Excellency the Lieutenant-Governor, Sir John Colborne, requesting him to procure for the United Presbytery of Upper Canada, the privilege of choosing a Professorship of Divinity in King's College to sit in the Council and in every respect to be on an equal footing with the other professors in the said college."[1]

The agitation thus begun continued for several years, though without any practical outcome. In 1837, the report of a Select Committee of the Legislative Council, which was afterwards adopted by the Council as a body, expressed itself as follows: "In order to reconcile all interests, your committee felt inclined to propose that a Theological Professor of the Church of Scotland should be placed on the foundation, as suggested by the Select Committee of the House of Commons in 1828; but, on further examination, it was found that the College Council has full power to do this without special enactment. Your committee therefore deemed it sufficient to recommend it to be done so soon after the College is put in operation as may be convenient."[2] This statement, it appears, was scarcely definite enough to satisfy the Presbyterians. The Honorable William Morris, their champion in the Legislative Council, in an open letter to the Reverend Dr. Strachan, expressed his fear that the fatal words "after" and "convenient" would "exclude during your (Dr. Strachan's) lifetime at least, the old-fashioned Geneva gown from the precincts of the College Avenue."[3]

The fears just expressed were apparently not without justification for in the measures which it took to give effect to the Charter Amendment Act of 1837, the College Council made no use of the discretionary powers which, in the opinion of the committee of the Legislative Council, it possessed. The plan of organization submitted by Dr. Strachan, the President of the College, to quote the language of one of the Presbyterian leaders of the time, "treated with contumelious silence, at once the recommendations of the Parent Government and the oft-expressed

---

[1]Dr Gregg, *Hist. of the Presbyterian Church in Canada*, p. 376.
[2]*Doc. Hist.*, Vol. IV, p. 90.
[3]Letter quoted in *Doc. Hist.*, Vol. III, p. 92.

wishes of the Colonists" (i. e. in favor of a Presbyterian Chair of Theology)."[1]

So doubtful were the Presbyterians of the intentions of the King's College Council that, in the latter part of the year 1837, a deputation (the Reverend Alexander Mathieson and the Reverend John Machar), representing Lower as well as Upper Canada, sought to enlist the aid of the Colonial Office in the securing of Presbyterian professorships of Theology both in King's College and in McGill College, Montreal. The Colonial Secretary, however, declined to interfere, on the ground that these were matters to be adjusted by the legislatures immediately concerned.

The matter under controversy came up for review again in 1839. In October of that year Sir George Arthur, the then Lieutenant-Governor, appointed a commission of which the Reverend Dr. McCaul (afterwards President of the University of Toronto) was chairman, "to examine into the past and present state of education throughout the Province and also to institute an enquiry with reference to the Constitution of King's College." This commission in its report expressed the conviction "that it would be wholly subversive of the order and well-being of an university to have within it chairs for the Professors of different denominations of religion." It recommended that, instead, the theological instruction needed by the various dissenting denominations should be given in theological seminaries of their own."[2]

This was the solution of the question which the Presbyterians were finally compelled by circumstances to adopt. In 1840, a Presbyterian institution, to be named the University of Kingston and to include a Theological Faculty of that denomination, was incorporated by an Act of the Provincial Legislature. The fifteenth section of this Act provided: "That so soon as the University of King's College, and the College thereby instituted, shall be in actual operation, it shall and may be lawful for the Governor, Lieutenant-Governor, or person administering the government of this Province, to authorize and direct the payment from the Funds of the said University of King's College,

---
[1] Letter of the Rev. Alexander Mathieson to Lord Glenelg, Colonial Secretary, dated Aug. 9th, 1837, in *Doc. Hist.*, Vol. III, p. 287.
[2] From Report of Commission, *Doc. Hist.*, Vol. IV, p. 92.

in aid of the College hereby instituted, of such yearly sum as to him shall seem just for the purpose of sustaining a Theological Professorship therein, and for the satisfaction of all claim on the part of the Church of Scotland for the institution of a Professorship of Divinity in the University of King's College, according to the faith and discipline of the Church of Scotland."[1]

Through an accident as peculiar as it was unforeseen the grant from the revenues of King's College provided for by the section just quoted, was never paid. In October, 1841, a Royal Charter was, upon petition, granted to the University of Kingston, and its name changed to Queen's College. This charter made no provision for a theological professorship and since it was held by the Law Officers of the Crown to have superseded wholly the Act of Incorporation of the preceding year, the authorities of King's College had a legal justification for withholding the grant in question. The strenuous protests of the injured parties did nothing, of course, to change the legal status of the case.

However, the Church of England was not long to retain its favored position in the matter of theological instruction at King's College. The University Act of 1849, besides changing the name of the College to the University of Toronto, completely secularized the institution. It was specifically enacted " That no Religious Test or qualification, whatsoever, shall be required of, or appointed for, any person admitted or matriculated, as a Member of such University, whether as a Scholar, Student, Fellow or otherwise, or of or for any person admitted to any Degree in any Art or Faculty, in the said University or of or for any person appointed to any Office, Professorship, Lectureship, Mastership, Tutorship or other place, or employment, whatsoever, in the same, nor shall Religious Observances according to the forms of any particular Religious Denomination, be imposed upon the Members, or Officers, of the said University or any of them."[2] In addition to the foregoing, other provisions required that the Chancellor should be a layman, that no degrees in Divinity should be granted and that the professorship in that subject should be abolished.

---

[1] *3rd Victoria, Chap. XXXV*, "An act to establish a College by the Name and Style of the Univ. of Kingston."
[2] *12th Victoria, Chap. LXXXII*, Sec. 29.

Thus in a little over twenty years' time an institution which began, to use the words of its founder, as a "Missionary College" of the Church of England, was transformed into a purely state institution which could claim the support and patronage of all the citizens of the Province, irrespective of their religious belief. Of the agitations in the press and from the pulpit, of the discussions and resolutions of both lay and religious organizations, of the parliamentary debates and enactments which contributed directly or indirectly to this transformation little more than a suggestion, however, has been given here.

CHAPTER IX. (*Supplementary.*)

EDUCATIONAL TENDENCIES IN ONTARIO, 1846–1906.

The progress of the Elementary Schools of Ontario during the last sixty years, and in a measure the progress of the schools of every rank, has been very closely identified with the efforts of one man, the Reverend Egerton Ryerson, Superintendent of Schools from 1846 till 1876. With the zeal of the missionary he combined the tireless energy of the captain of industry and the constructive genius of the statesman. In his general policy he displayed to a marked degree the ability of knowing "the season when to take occasion by the hand and make the bounds of freedom wider yet."

Being defeated in 1850 in his efforts to make the public schools entirely free, he waited for over twenty years till public sentiment, as expressed in the provincial legislature, should come to his way of thinking. His attitude and behavior during this interval is thus described by one who was his co-worker during the whole period of his incumbency of office. "The practical mind of Dr. Ryerson at once saw that the American idea of free schools was the true one. He moreover perceived that by giving his countrymen facilities for freely discussing the question among the rate payers once a year, they would educate themselves into the idea without any interference from the state. These facilities were provided in 1850 and for twenty years the question of free schools as against rate-bill schools (fees, etc.) was discussed every January in from three thousand to five thousand school sections until free schools became voluntarily the rule and rate-bill schools the exception."[1]

To this policy of public self-education, Dr. Ryerson added an active propaganda of his own. "I propose," he remarked in his report to the Government in 1846, "to visit and employ one or two days in school discourse and deliberation with the Superintendent, visitors, trustees and teachers in each of the several Districts of Upper Canada. I know of no means so effectual to remove prejudice, to create unanimity of views and

---

[1]Prefatory note by Dr. J. G. Hodgins. In *Ryerson Memorial Volume*, p. IV.

feelings, and to excite a general interest in the course of public education.[1] As has been already mentioned, Dr Ryerson's plans for the improvement of the elementary schools took permanent shape in the School Act of 1871. The chief provisions of this act were as follows:

(1) The schools were made entirely free through the abolition of the rate-bills and fees which had hitherto been allowed.

(2) Every child of school age was required to be in attendance at school during at least four months of the year.

(3) County inspectors of sufficient qualifications to satisfy the Council of Public Instruction, took the place of the local superintendents. These inspectors could be removed only for misconduct or inefficiency.

(4) Provision was made for uniform examinations throughout the Province for promotion from the elementary school to the high school.

For several years prior to 1876 Dr. Ryerson had sought to be relieved of the rather onerous duties of his office. One reason for this desire was a belief that the head of the public school system of the Province should be more closely in touch with the provincial legislature. To this end he suggested the appointment of a Minister of Education who should be a member of the Provincial Legislature as well as of the Provincial Cabinet, and who should be the exponent of the educational policy of his party on the floor of the House. Upon Dr. Ryerson's retirement this change was effected and for nearly thirty years the affairs of the Education Department were in the hands of a Minister of Education who ranked with the other ministers of the Crown, and whose continuance in office depended upon the ability of his party to command a majority at the polls. Quite recently, however, an important change has been made in this connection. It was felt that it was too much to expect one man to combine the functions of the political leader with those of the educational expert. Consequently there has been created (or rather re-created) by a recent act of the provincial legislature the office of Superintendent of Education with duties partly administrative and partly advisory. This office is subordinate to that of Minister of Education, and is expected to

---

[1]*Ryerson Memorial Volume*, p. 82.

increase the efficiency of the latter official by bringing him into close and constant touch with the most recent educational ideas and practices.

To adequately describe the progress that has taken place during the last fifty years within the elementary schools themselves would need several chapters each of considerable length. In the few paragraphs which can be devoted to the topic here, the best that can be done perhaps, is to indicate briefly what the schools were at the beginning and what they are at the end of the period mentioned, and to attempt to determine the chief forces which wrought the change.

It would appear that in 1850 the schools in question differed little from those of twenty years before, and which have already been described in detail. Dr. J. H. Sangster, a teacher of the period, a graduate, and later the principal, of the Provincial Normal School, alludes to this fact in the following words: "Fifty years ago the youth of our fair Province were not overburdened with educational privileges. Upper Canada College and a few widely scattered Grammar Schools afforded moderate educational opportunities to children of the favored class, but the common schools even in cities and towns were in most instances so mean in appearance and so wretched in character and appointment, and so barren in useful results, that private schools of a scarcely higher grade were patronized by all save the miserably poor."[1]

In speaking of the text-books, Dr. Sangster informed his hearers that the "outfit of an entire school would not infrequently consist of a few testaments, a Gough's or a Walkinghame's arithmetic, and a Mavor's spelling book. Haply, ff the school were above the ordinary run, or had any special claim of literary excellence, a chance copy of Fox's Book of Martyrs or the Spectator or of Baldwin's 'Pantheon' might be found in the highest reading class, the single book passing in succession to each reader and the long words being skipped as being equally unpronounceable by both teacher and taught."

As has been suggested, the energy of Dr. Ryerson and the leavening influences of the agencies he set at work—notably

---

[1] From address at the Jubilee celebration of the Provincial Normal School, Toronto, included in the *Ryerson Memorial Volume*.

the normal school—gradually effected a revolution. The log school house, with its unsanitary and uninviting interior, gave place to the more suitable building of frame, brick or stone, with equipment more in keeping with the needs of its inmates. The emigrant adventurer and the discharged soldier gave way to the young man, or more often to the young woman, who possessed in addition to youthful energy and approved moral character, the academic and professional training represented by a normal school course. Consequently the public school as an institution came to deserve and to enjoy the patronage of all classes in the community.

The statesmanlike breadth which characterized Dr. Ryerson's administration of his office, and which slighted not the least of the details which might make for efficiency, still characterizes in the main the regulations by means of which the Education Department seeks to maintain a uniformly high standard throughout the schools of the Province. Not only are such matters as the certification and inspection of teachers and the general organization of school programs provided for, but careful and minute instructions are given about such matters as the furniture and equipment of the school house, the text-books to be used, everything, it would appear, down to the location of the school pump. In the matter of examinations, and there are many of these, specific instructions are given as to the place and hours of examination in each subject, the precautions to be used by presiding examiners, even the number of marks to be deducted for each mis-spelled word in the papers examined. So complete indeed is the system, so carefully is every contingency provided for, that the observer, accustomed to the greater freedom and opportunity for local and individual initiative prevalent in most states of the Union, is apt to feel that its completeness is perhaps its greatest defect.

The district grammar school of 1850 was apparently a very different institution from the high school of the present day. In the first place it taught, as did the grammar school of the earlier period, the elementary as well as the higher branches, thus, to quote the words of Dr. Ryerson, "impairing its own efficiency and that of the neighboring common schools."[1] In

---
[1] *Journal of Education*, Vol. II, (1849), p. 168.

the second place it did not articulate with the higher institutions of learning. From the thirty to forty grammar schools existing in 1849 only eight students matriculated in that year in the provincial university.[1]

The Grammar School Act of 1853 sought to remedy this and other defects. By it a grant of £100 was made to the senior grammar school in each county. The remainder of the income from the grammar school fund was to be divided among the various counties in proportion to their population. School buildings were to be erected and maintained by a county rate. The course of study was to include the higher branches of an English and Commercial education, the elements of natural philosophy and mechanics, and the Latin and Greek languages so far as to prepare students for the University of Toronto. The program of studies and the general rules and regulations were to be prescribed by the Council of Public Instruction for Upper Canada and approved by the governor in council. It was a part of the duty of every senior master to make observations on the weather and to keep a meteorological journal. The necessary instruments for this work were to be provided at the expense of the municipality in which the school was situated.[2]

In 1871 the name "high school" was formally applied to those institutions which had theretofore been known as grammar schools, the course of study was enlarged to include French and German, and provision was made for the establishment of a superior class of high school to be known as collegiate institutes. These latter schools were required to have at least four masters, each of whom was to have special qualifications as an instructor in the branches assigned to him. Subsequent legislation has raised the standard of qualifications for high school teachers and has imposed certain minimum requirements as regards building and equipment.

The high schools of the present day are kept closely in touch with the Education Department through the various departmental examinations conducted annually, and at which a large number of high school students are candidates for diplomas, and through the work of the high school inspectors who are salaried officers of the department and whose reports have a great deal to do

---
[1] *Ibid.*
[2] Appendix E to *Report of Superintendent of Public Instruction* for 1853.

in determining the attitude of the Department towards individual schools. As in the elementary schools, the high school courses of study and the text-books to be used are all prescribed by the Department.

The high schools, though admitting all students who can pass the entrance examination, and though controlled to a large degree by a popularly elected school board, are not all free schools. As is shown in the statistical table given at the end of the chapter a considerable part of the revenues of these schools is derived from fees. There is a slight general tendency towards the abolition of fees either wholly or in the case of resident students. However, some sixty per cent of the high schools of the Province still require fees of their students.[1]

The need for some provision for the professional training of teachers early engaged the attention of Dr. Ryerson. During the first of his visits abroad he had occasion to study the normal schools of Prussia, and of other continental countries. During a brief sojourn in the United States he had also opportunity to study the working of the Normal School at Albany, New York, then recently founded. The result of all this was the establishment in 1847 of a Normal School at Toronto, the capital of the Province. Shortly afterwards, seven and a half acres of land were purchased as a site, and in 1851 the cornerstone of a commodious building was laid with appropriate ceremonies. Dr. Ryerson's conception of the close relation of religion to the work of teaching is illustrated in an inscription, composed by himself, which was placed upon this stone " This Institution, erected by the Enlightened Liberality of Parliament, is Designed for the Instruction and Training of School Teachers upon Christian Principles."[2]

That Dr. Ryerson's efforts to establish a normal school were not sympathetically received in all quarters is illustrated by the following extract from a memorial sent to the Provincial Legislature in 1847 by the Gore District Council. After a reference to the school in question as entirely unsuited to a country like Canada, the statement is made, " Nor do your memorialists hope to provide qualified teachers by any other means in the present

---
[1] See *Report of the Minister of Education* for 1905, Vol. II, p. 39.
[2] *Ryerson Memorial Volume*, p. 87.

circumstances of the country than securing as heretofore the services of those whose physical disabilities from age render this mode of obtaining a livelihood the only one suited to their decaying energies, or by employing such of the newly arrived emigrants as are qualified for common school teachers, year by year as they come amongst us, and who will adopt this as a means of temporary support until their character and ability are known and turned to better account for themselves." This memorandum was sent to the various district councils of the Province with the hope of securing their concurrence.

The Colborne District Council, however, took direct issue with the arguments just quoted, in the following language, " Nor can your Committee reconcile it either with their sense of duty to rest satisfied with the services of those whose physical disabilities from age and decaying energies render them unfit, or of those ' newly arrived emigrants ' whose ' unknown character and abilities ' render them unable to procure a livelihood by any other means than by becoming the preceptors of our children, the dictators of their sentiments and manners, the guardians of their virtues, and in a high degree the masters of their future destinies in this world and the next." Much to the credit of the enlightened sentiment of the Province as a whole, the attitude of the Colborne District Council was eventually the more popular one, though the reforms for which Dr. Ryerson stood so zealously were at times seriously imperiled. So closely did his opponents press him at one time (1849) that he tendered his resignation. Fortunately for the future welfare of the Province, the resignation was not accepted and in the following year compromise legislation was effected whereby his political enemies were appeased without the sacrifice of the essential reforms for which he stood.

For many years the normal school gave academic as well as professional instruction. Finally, however, in 1871, it was felt that the county grammar schools or high schools as they came to be called, were entirely adequate for the academic training of teachers. Since that time, consequently, the work of the normal school has been confined to the giving of professional courses and to the furnishing of opportunity for practice work by the teacher in training. The growth of the school system made necessary the establishment in 1875 of a second normal school at Ottawa in the Eastern part of the Province. Subsequently a third school was opened at London in Western Ontario.

The work of these three schools is practically identical. The requirements for admission are the same—the obtaining of a non-professional certificate of a certain specified character at the yearly departmental examinations and at least one year of successful teaching upon a third grade professional certificate obtained in a manner to be described shortly. At the outset the required term of attendance was a half-year, but it was subsequently lengthened to one year. The fact that the Roman Catholic Separate Schools are an important factor in the public school system, numerically and otherwise, has been recognized, though not in any formal way, by the maintenance for many years of a member of that Communion at the head of the Ottawa Normal School. Under the present regulation the successful completion of a year's work at a Normal School brings to the candidate a second class professional certificate which conveys a permanent right to teach in the elementary schools of the Province.

A professional school of a higher grade is the Ontario Normal College, situated at Hamilton and established in the early nineties primarily for the purpose of training teachers for the high schools and collegiate institutes of the Province. In this institution as in those already mentioned, professional courses are given and practice teaching is required. The requirements for admission are senior leaving standing (roughly speaking, the equivalent of one year's work in college) or graduation in arts from any university in the British dominions. Upon the satisfactory completion of a year's work, certificates are granted varying in character with the academic acquirements possessed by the student.

The maintenance of an institution such as the Normal College apart from the Provincial University has for many years been felt to be a mistake. In consequence of this feeling provision was recently made by an Act of the Provincial Legislature for the transforming of the institution in question into a department of education in the University. Such a department has recently been organized and a Professor of Education chosen.

The Model School as it at present exists seems to be an institution peculiar to the Province of Ontario. Its history may be briefly indicated as follows: In 1843 permission was given to the municipal authorities of any county to raise by county-rate a sum not exceeding £200 and to expend the same in the maintenance of a County Model School. The purpose of this school was to be the instruction of persons already engaged in the work of teaching who were desirous of further perfecting themselves in their art. The School Act of 1846 sought to promote the efficiency of these schools by requiring that their teachers should be graduates of the Normal School and that their students should be granted certificates upon an examination by the District Superintendent.

This early legislation was apparently ineffective, for in a circular letter addressed in 1850 to the chief municipal authority in each township (the reeve) Dr. Ryerson asserted, "The attempts of district councils to establish model schools have thus far proved entire failures." The educational legislation of 1850 sought to remedy the evil by placing the schools under township authority. This change, however, brought little improvement. In 1871, with the appointment of County Inspector of Schools, came a marked improvement in the Model Schools. Under the competent supervision thus provided they proved of decided value in furnishing to the beginners in the teaching profession a modicum of professional training and of actual teaching experience. Up to the present time the model school in each county has been attached to the public school in some village or town. The principal of the school in question, has, as a rule, been the principal of the model school. The course has occupied the four months from September till December inclusive, and the requirements for admission, the instruction to be given, and the details of the management have been prescribed in detail by the Provincial Department of Education. Upon the satisfactory completion of the work and the passing of the prescribed examination, the student has been granted a third class professional certificate which entitles him to teach in the elementary schools of the Province for three years.

The Model School has for some years, however, been regarded as little better than a makeshift. Recently the Provincial Government has undertaken to more than double the number of normal schools with a view to an eventual total discontinuance of the Model School as a part of the provincial educational system. This movement is thus described and justified in a recent circular from the Minister of Education:

> To increase the efficiency of the teachers, the Government is also providing an improved system of professional training in the form of three additional Normal Schools for old Ontario and one for new Ontario, at a capital cost of more than $250,000, and an increase of the yearly expenditure for maintenance of more than $60,000. With the addition of a Faculty of Education in the Provincial University, which has now been arranged for, we shall have, in a couple of years, a complete and modern system of training for all grades of teachers. The new scheme of professional training will provide for two main grades of Public School teacher certificates, First Class and Second Class. The work for First Class Teachers and High School Assistants will be taken up in the new Faculty of Education in Toronto University; that for Second Class in the reorganized Normal Schools. It is, however, intended to provide in addition for the less advanced counties in Old Ontario and the poorer parts of the districts, teachers with qualifications corresponding to those of the old Third Class certificates (Primary non-professional). The professional work for these certificates will be taken up in a few Model Schools which will be retained for the purpose and made thoroughly efficient. Such certificates will, of course, be confined to the counties and districts concerned, and it is hoped will gradually disappear.

The development of the Provincial University after its secularization in 1849 has been mainly along two different lines. (1) An enlargement of the curriculum and the provision of professional courses to keep pace with the marked scientific and industrial progress of the age. (2) An effort to secure the affiliation of the other higher institutions of learning in the Province with a view to making the University the sole examining and degree conferring body (for the higher degrees at least) in the Province. There is occasion here to speak of (2) only.

The movement towards the centralization of the higher education of the Province has been slow and hesitating and with various counteracting tendencies from time to time. Even at the present time it is far from complete, although important steps in that direction have been taken in recent years.

According to one historian of the Canadian universities, "One object in view in the (University) legislation of 1849 was to secure the abandonment by the denominational colleges of their

University powers and to obtain their co-operation with the Provincial Universities in the promotion of secular culture."[1]

The University Act of 1853 sought to further prepare the way for the union referred to by divesting the University of Toronto of all teaching functions and vesting the latter in a new institution known as University College. The model consulted in this movement was the University of London which, itself a secular institution, was planned to act as an examining and degree conferring body for various "teaching" colleges. In the Act in question provision was made for the affiliation with the university of the different denominational universities then in existence. The different colleges in question (with the exception of Trinity University then recently established by Dr. Strachan) did actually enter into the relationship mentioned, but "it is not known that they ever sent up a student for examination,"[2] and in a few years the attendance of the heads of these outside institutions at the meetings of the University Senate began to diminish and shortly decreased altogether.

There soon developed in the denominational school, instead of a spirit of co-operation, a spirit of open hostility to the Provincial University. This spirit showed itself in repeated attacks on the University management—attacks which led to the appointment of a Parliamentary Committee of Inquiry which eventually gave way to a Commission. This Commission in its report recommended various reforms in the financial management of the University and a yearly grant to the four denominational schools (Queen's, Victoria, Regiopolis and Trinity) of $10,000 a year with the understanding that the University of Toronto should prescribe for them their curricula, conduct their examinations, and grant their degrees. Nothing was done either by the Legislature or by the Government in regard to this report, with the exception of an increase to $5,000 a year of the annual grant allowed the outlying colleges by the legislature. In 1869 the annual grant just mentioned was withdrawn and the denominational schools compelled to look to private sources for their support. This, it would appear, was a blessing in disguise, since it led to the beginning of a vigorous and independent life such as they had never known before. In a few years their

---
[1] Dr. Burwash in Paper read at meeting of Royal Soc. of Canada, 1904.
[2] Ibid.

income from voluntary endowment was greater than had ever been received from the public treasury.

In 1883 the growth of the provincial university had made the income from endowment decidedly inadequate. The consequent application to the Provincial Legislature for aid provoked strenuous opposition on the part of the denominational college and led to the revival of the "University Federation" scheme. After considerable deliberation the plan of federation adopted was essentially as follows:

(1) The heads of the various federating institutions were to be members of the University Senate. Each college was to have one other representative and the professors of each college to have two representatives.

(2) The University was to assume certain teaching functions and provide instruction in Pure Mathematics, Physics, Astronomy, Geology, Mineralogy, Chemistry (pure and applied), Zoology, Botany, Physiology, Ethnology (including Comparative Philology), History, Logic, and Metaphysics, History of Philosophy, Italian and Spanish, Political Economy and Civil Politics, Jurisprudence, Constitutional Law, and such other sciences, arts and branches of knowledge as the Senate of the Provincial University might from time to time determine. The remaining subjects of the curriculum were to be in the hands of University College as one of the federating institutions and such other colleges as might become members of the University.

The principle which guided the division of work was, according to a competent authority (Chancellor Burwash of Victoria University), "that the University should take the sciences, including History and Political Science and the colleges Philosophy and Literature. The reasons for this general division were twofold, on the side of the University, which was to be supported by the state, the sciences furnished the knowledge provided for industrial and political life, and were thus a reasonable matter of public provision. On the side of the colleges, philosophy and literature furnished material of culture and moral and ethical development and thus afforded them the best field for their special work—that of culture and the moral side of education." After some seven years of discussion and conflict within the Methodist Church itself the General Conference of 1890 voted in favor of federation and in November the final stage in the process was completed by the proclamations of the Lieutenant-Governor federating Victoria University with the University of Toronto.

The University Act of 1901, besides making material changes in the constitution of the University, made special provision for the admission of Trinity University into federation and thus a schism of over half a century was healed.

The Provincial University as at present constituted consists of the three federating Colleges in Arts—University College, Victoria and Trinity; two professional faculties, Medicine and Applied Sciences and Engineering; thirteen professional schools—five in Theology, two in Music, and one each in Law, Pedagogy, Agriculture, Dentistry, Pharmacy, and Veterinary Surgery.

The higher institutions of learning which yet remain outside of federation, and will probably do so for many years to come, are Queen's University at Kingston, a flourishing institution under the control of the Presbyterian Church, McMaster University at Toronto, a Baptist institution, Western University at London, under Anglican control, and Ottawa University, a Roman Catholic Institution, situated at the Dominion Capital.

The first mentioned of these schools has within recent years received financial aid from the provincial government on the ground that the furnishing of higher education along secular lines is a public service which demands public recognition and support even if the institution furnishing this education is not under public control.

To return to the subject of the Provincial University and to conclude this brief, and hence imperfect summary, it may be in order to quote a statement from an authoritative source of the principles which have guided in the federation movement and the results which have thus far been achieved.

Finally in this common work federation has made the State, the Christian Church, and private enterprise and liberality all mutually helpful to each other on the sound basis of mutual independence. Public funds have very largely provided for the Central University, University College, and the School of Practical Science at an outlay of over $4,000,000 on capital account, and an annual expenditure of about $180,000.

Professional enterprise maintains the faculty of medicine at an annual cost of $64,000. The Agricultural and Normal Colleges are sustained by the state at an annual expenditure of nearly $100,000. The other affiliated professional schools are all the result of private or professional enterprise and have involved a capital outlay of $300,000. The other colleges and theological schools are the creation of the churches and represent in capital over $3,000,000 and an annual expenditure of over $100,000.

The University of Toronto on the federation principle represents to the people of Ontario a combined capital of over $7,000,000 and an annual expenditure of nearly $500,000 for the higher education of over 3000 students drawn from all parts of the county and Dominion and even from China, Japan, India and Africa, and from Newfoundland and the West Indies.*

---

* Paper on the history of the University of Toronto, read by Chancellor Burwash at the meeting of the Royal Society of Canada, 1904.

HIGH SCHOOL STATISTICS.*

	1854.	1864.	1874.	1884.	1894.	1904.
Population............................	950,551 in 1852	1,396,091 in 1860	1,620,851 in 1870	1,913,460 in 1880	2,114,321 in 1890	2,215,854 in 1900
Number of schools...................	64	95	108	106	129	138
Number of pupils attending school...	4,287	5,589	7,871	12,737	23,523	27,709
Number of High School teachers.....	99	139	248	358	554	661
Amount of Legislative Grant.........	$21,939	$45,604	$76,874	$85,206	$100,000.00	$120,799.49
Amount of municipal school grant and assessments......................	17,496	35,266	156,826	220,668	423,296.27	506,005.41
Other receipts (Fees, etc.)..........	11,618	9,974	65,260	102,103	217,354.91	244,062.75
Total income from all sources...	$51,053	$90,844	$298,960	$407,977	$740,651.18	$960,867.00
Paid teachers' salaries..............	$43,490	$73,258	$179,046	$282,776	$507,441.63	$620,710.00
Paid for sites, buildings and repairs.	3,404	6,139	63,684	34,013	48,159.95	50,512.00
Other expenditures..................	139	6,419	42,963	68,637	132,830.64	205,865.00
Total expenditures...............	$47,033	$85,816	$286,593	$385,426	$688,532.22	$877,087.00

* Compiled from various reports of the Minister of Education.

COMMON SCHOOL STATISTICS, INCLUDING THOSE OF SEPARATE SCHOOLS.*

	1844.	1854.	1864.	1874.	1884.	1894.	1904.
Population of Ontario............	506,055 in 1842	950,551 in 1850	1,396,091 in 1860	1,620,851 in 1870	1,913,460 in 1880	2,114,321 in 1890	2,215,854 in 1900
Number of schools...............	2,610	3,224	4,225	4,758	5,316	5,987	6,177
School population between 5 and 16	183,539	277,922	425,565	511,603	471,287	593,840	576,537
Number of pupils attending school	96,756	204,168	371,695	464,047	466,917	between 5 & 21 483,723	between 5 & 21 444,621
Number of school teachers:							
Male..........................		2,508	3,011	2,601	2,789	2,800	2,075
Female........................		1,031	1,614	3,135	4,296	6,029	7,479
Amount of Legislative grant.....	$80,000	$90,690	$177,053	$267,772	$267,084	$299,217	$405,361 71
Amount of Municipal grant and assessments....................	66,890	483,523	1,023,400	2,214,976	2,675,721	3,460,328 71	4,464,227 14
Trustees' rate bills and other receipts.........................	89,339	252,339	283,734	756,523	1,047,417	1,212,961 53	1,600,982 60
Total income from all sources	$236,229	$826,552	$1,484,187	$3,239,271	$3,990,222	$4,972,507 24	$6,470,571 45
Paid teachers' salaries..........	$206,856	$578,868	$996,956	$1,647,750	$2,296,027	$2,847,731 10	$3,473,710 54
Paid for sites, buildings and repairs		115,311	153,059	853,584	907,102	445,386 71	578,655 68
Other expenditures..............		88,312	135,303	363,998	17,733	955,013 74	1,407,127 36
Total expenditures.........	$782,491	$1,285,318	$2,865,332	$3,280,862	$4,248,131 55	$5,459,493 58	

*Compiled from various reports of the Minister of Education.

BIBLIOGRAPHY (PARTIAL) OF WORKS CONSULTED IN PREPARING THE FOREGOING.

BABY, W. L. Souvenirs of the Past; an instructive and amusing work giving an account of the customs and the habits of the pioneers of Upper Canada. Windsor, Ontario, 1896.

BONNYCASTLE, SIR R. H. The Canadas in 1841. London, H. Colburn, 1842.

BOURINOT, SIR J. G. The Intellectual Development of the Canadian People. Toronto, Hunter, Rose & Co., 1881.

BRYMNER, DOUGLAS. Reports of Dominion Archivist. 1884-1900.

BURWASH, NATHANIEL, D. D., LL. D. Egerton Ryerson. In Makers of Canada Series. Toronto, George N. Morang & Co., 1903.

CANNIFF, WILLIAM. History of the Settlement of Upper Canada. Toronto, Dudley & Burns, 1869.

DENT, J. C., and SCADDING, REV. H., D. D. Semi-Centennial Memorial Volume. Toronto, Past and Present.

FIDLER, G. Observations on Professions, Literature, Manners and Emigration in the United States and Canada Made During a Residence there in 1832. New York, J. & J. Harper, 1833.

GREGG, REV. WILLIAM, D. D. A Short History of the Presbyterian Church in the Dominion of Canada from the Earliest Times till 1884. Toronto, The Author, 1892.

HAIGHT, CANNIFF. Country Life in Canada Fifty Years Ago. Personal recollections and reminiscences of a sexagenarian. Toronto, Hunter, Rose & Co., 1885.

HODGINS, J. GEORGE, LL. D. Documentary History of Education in Upper Canada. 13 vols. 1792-1855. Printed as supplements to various reports of the Minister of Education for Ontario.

HODGINS, J. GEORGE, LL. D. The Ryerson Memorial Volume, 1889. Toronto, Warwick & Sons, 1889.

HOPKINS, J. CASTELL, ED. Canada — An Encyclopedia of the Country. Vol. IV, Sec. 3. The Universities and higher educational system of Canada.

JOURNAL OF EDUCATION, THE. First volume, 1848, published by Dr. Ryerson in connection with the office of Superintendent of Public Instruction.

KINGSFORD, W. The History of Canada. 1608-1841. 10 vols. Toronto, Rowsell & Hutchinson, 1887-1898.

LINDSEY, CHARLES. Life and Times of William Lyon Mackenzie.

LIZARS, R. and K. M. In the Days of the Canada Company. The settlement of the Huron Tract and a view of the social life of the period, 1825-1850.

MACKENZIE, WILLIAM LYON. Sketches of Canada and the United States. London, Effingham Wilson, 1833.

MACKENZIE, WILLIAM LYON. Seventh Report on Grievances, 1832. Toronto, M. Reynolds.

MAC MULLEN, J. The History of Canada. Brockville, McMullen & Co., 1868.

MESSAGE from His Excellency the Lieutenant-Governor, of 30th Jan., 1836, transmitting a despatch from His Majesty's Government. Printed by order of the Honorable, the Legislative Council. Toronto, R. Stanton, Printer.

MORGAN, HENRY JAMES. Sketches of Celebrated Canadians and Persons Connected with Canada from the Earliest Period in the History of the Province down to the Present Time. Quebec, Hunter, Rose & Co., 1862.

OGDEN, JOHN COSENS. A Tour through Upper and Lower Canada. By a citizen of the United States. Litchfield, Conn., 1799.

PRESTON, T. R. Three Years' Residence in Canada, from 1837 to 1839. London, R. Bentley, 1840.

PROCEEDINGS of the Royal Society of Canada, 1904. Article by Nathaniel Burwash, D. D., LL. D., on the History of the University of Toronto.

REPORT and Despatches of the Earl of Durham, Her Majesty's High Commissioner and Governor-General of British North America. London, 1839.

REPORT of a Select Committee upon the complaint contained in an address to the King from the House of Assembly, passed 15th April, 1835. Toronto, R. Stanton, 1836.

REPORTS of the Education Department of Ontario, 1845-1905.

ROGER, C. The Rise of Canada from Barbarism to Wealth and Civilization. Quebec, P. Sinclair, 1856.

ROLPH, DR. THOMAS. A Brief Account with Observations on the West Indies, with a Statistical Account of Upper Canada. Dundas, U. C. 1836.

ROSS, HON. G. W. LL. D. The School System of Ontario. In Internat. Ed. Series. D. Appleton & Co.

RYERSON, REVEREND EGERTON. The Royalists of America and Their Times. Toronto, William Briggs, 1880.

RYERSON, REVEREND EGERTON. The Story of My Life. Being reminiscences of sixty years in the public service in Canada. Toronto, William Briggs, 1883.

SCADDING, REVEREND HENRY, D. D. Toronto of Old. Collections and recollections illustrative of the early settlement and social life of the capital of Ontario.

SMITH, M. A Geographical View of the British Possessions in North America. Baltimore, P. Munro, for the Author, 1814.

STATUTES of various sessions of the Provincial Parliament of Upper Canada. 1792–1841.

STRICKLAND, S. Twenty-seven Years in Canada West, or the Experience of an Old Settler. Edited by A. Strickland. London, R. Bentley, 1853.

TALBOT, E. A. Five Years' Residence in the Canadas. London, Longman, Hurst & Co., 1824.

TAYLOR, FENNINGS. The Last Three Bishops Appointed by the Crown for the Anglican Church in Canada. Montreal, John Lovell, 1869.

THELLER, E. A. Canada in 1837–1838, showing the cause of the late attempted revolution and its failure, the present condition of the people and their future prospects, etc. 2 vols. Philadelphia, H. F. Amers, 1841.

TIMPERLAKE, J. Toronto, Past and Present. Toronto, Peter A. Goss, 1877.

TRAILL, MRS. C. P. S. The Backwoods of Canada, being letters from the wife of an emigrant officer. London, C. Knight, 1836.